Debating Culture

Debating Culture

Anirban Ganguly

DK PRINTWORLD
Publishers of Indian Traditions

Cataloging in Publication Data — DK
[Courtesy: D.K. Agencies (P) Ltd. <docinfo@dkagencies.com>]

Ganguly, Anirban.
Debating culture/Anirban Ganguly.
p. cm.
Includes bibliographical references (p.).
ISBN 9788124607039

1. India – Civilization. 2. Intellectuals – India. I. Title.

DDC 954 23

ISBN 13: 978-81-246-0703-9 (HB)
ISBN 13: 978-81-246-0704-6 (PB)
First published in India in 2013

Printed and published by:
D.K. Printworld (P) Ltd.
Regd. Office : *'Vedaśrī,'* F-395, Sudarshan Park
(Metro Station: Ramesh Nagar)
New Delhi – 110 015
Phones : (011) 2545 3975, 2546 6019; *Fax* : 2546 5926
e-mail : indology@dkprintworld.com
Web : www.dkprintworld.com

Swami Vivekananda
who dynamized the debate

&

Sri Aurobindo
who enriched it

Foreword

OPEN the yellowed tomes authored by a few Western Indologists of the nineteenth or early twentieth centuries — say, Stella Kramrisch, John Woodroffe, Sylvain Lévi, Louis Renou or Jean Filliozat — and you will find, to quote the last two, "the same comprehension, the same admiration of Indian civilization". A comprehension based on a thorough study and discussion of the fundamentals of Indian culture, her thought and belief systems, her aesthetics and spirituality, her social or technological achievements. This is precisely the kind of discussion that is so rare in today's India, as if those fundamentals should be of interest only to ageing scholars sitting in musty libraries.

Most of the prominent Indian intellectuals of the day confirm this impression: note, for instance, how the historian Ramachandra Guha, in his recent *Makers of Modern India*, has no use for either Swami Vivekananda or Sri Aurobindo, thereby implying that their comprehensive exposition and discussion of what makes India "India" is of no relevance to our "modern" nation.

Also absent from Guha's collection are the other great figures of India's renaissance that Anirban Ganguly chooses to focus on, with one exception: Nehru is the odd man out here, but the chapter dedicated to him is welcome as it brings out little-known aspects of his concern for India's cultural heritage. Nevertheless, he cannot be regarded, as nearly all the others can, as a major player in the twentieth-century continuation of the cultural renaissance that swept through India in reaction to the crushing dominance of the colonial rulers.

Whether he explores Swami Vivekananda, A.K. Coomaraswamy, Sister Nivedita or K.M. Munshi, Anirban Ganguly displays a flair for picking out the most stimulating of their thoughts on issues ranging from aesthetics, artistic sensitivity or, national education to cultural integration — in a word, what constitutes Indian identity. There is a lurking suspicion that as a nation, we will be time and again forced by circumstances to return to those essential questions. Our prominent intellectuals are confident of having once and for all relegated them to some dark cellar, with neat labels of "nationalism", "exclusivism" or even "chauvinism" stuck on them as on dinosaur bones, but they forget that things in India move on a longer time-scale and that these issues will not leave us, because they are in us.

Also, they do not realize that the thinkers presented here were, in fact, far more inclusive than they themselves are, but insisted on a clear foundation for Indian identity. Today's rallying cry is for "many identities", which is of course fine as far as it goes, but without such a clear foundation — in effect, a mosaic rather than a banyan tree. Time will tell which model is more sustainable; in the meantime, the thinkers presented here will continue to water the ancient banyan; let us see whether it can still sprout new shoots.

Michel Danino

Contents

Acknowledgement

I AM grateful to K.C. Ajit Doval, Director, Vivekananda International Foundation, New Delhi for encouraging me to write this book. I am grateful to Michel Danino, scholar of Indian culture and chronicler of "The Lost River" for having agreed to write the Foreword in spite of his multifarious research and teaching commitments. My appreciations are also due to the staff of the general reading room and the manuscript section of the Nehru Memorial Museum & Library, New Delhi for their proactive facilitation of my work with prompt supply of documents and references.

I also thank Susheel K. Mittal of D.K. Printworld for having shown interest in the work and for deciding to publish it.

Being convinced of the relevance of this book, Anuttama, my wife persistently goaded me into overcoming my diffidence. My gratitude, as always, to her!

Introduction

ANALYSING the "Deeper Meaning of the Struggle" for Indian independence, scholar and interpreter of Indian culture Ananda Coomaraswamy (1877–1947) made a very poignant observation that continues to hold great relevance. Referring to a deeper dimension of the Indian nationalist movement, Coomaraswamy argued:

> Five hundred years hence it will matter little to humanity whether a few Indians more or less, have held official posts in India, or a few million bales of cloth been manufactured in Bombay or Lancashire factories; but it will matter much whether the great ideals of Indian culture have been carried forward or allowed to die. It is with these that Indian Nationalism is essentially concerned, and upon these that the fate of India as a nation depends.[1]

His essential argument was that there could be "no true realization of political unity until Indian life [was] again inspired by the unity of the national culture".[2] Coomaraswamy called for the nationalist movement to direct its effort towards unraveling the marvels of Indian culture and towards seeking national strength from its varied dimensions. For him the "vital forces associated with the national movement in India" were "not merely political, but moral, literary and artistic",[3] the regeneration of India had to come through her arts and "not

---

1 Ananda Coomaraswamy, *Essays in National Idealism*, 1909, pp. 1-2.

2 Ibid., p. iii.

3 Ibid., p. iv.

by politics and economics alone".[4] In short, Coomaraswamy seemed to point at the necessity of realizing the intrinsic and unifying strengths of Indian culture and of accepting these in the mainstream of the national movement. He lamented the loss of beauty and of its appreciation from the national life saying that "India, above all nations, was beautiful once" and that too not long ago. Thus Coomaraswamy's was a case for the centrality of culture in India's national life.

In the past, especially during the early phase of the nationalist movement, the debate on the place and the role of culture in our national life was robust and varied. It saw a number of stalwart thought-leaders pitching in. One of Coomaraswamy's contemporary in the cultural field, the poet-laureate Rabindranath Tagore, on his part, also made a strong case for developing a "complete and moving orb of Indian culture"[5] that shall act as a strong centripetal force. In his address on "The Centre of Indian Culture" delivered at Madras in 1919, Tagore dwelt on the necessity of rediscovering our cultural past, of making a robust use of it in the present times and of eradicating the Indian mentality which habitually saw itself as a "disinherited people". "If we are to create a centre of Indian culture", he argued, "we must start with the belief that India has a culture, and one which is worthy of being imparted to all."[6] He cautioned against the tendency of being "insularly modern". Observed Tagore:

> There are some who are insularly modern, who believe that the past is the bankrupt time, leaving no assets for us, but only a legacy of debts. They refuse to believe that the army

[4] Coomaraswamy, *Art and Swadeshi*, 1911, pp. 3-4.

[5] Rabindranath Tagore, "The Centre of Indian Culture", in S.K. Das, ed., *The English Writings of Rabindranath Tagore (EWRT)*, vol. 2, 2008, p. 482. Tagore delivered the lecture on 9 February 1919 at Madras at the invitation of Annie Besant (1847–1933).

[6] Ibid., p. 483.

> that is marching forward can be fed from the rear. It is well to remind them that the great ages of renaissance in history were those when men suddenly discovered the seeds of thought in the granary of the past.
>
> The unfortunate people, who have lost the harvest of their past, have lost their present age. They have missed their seeds for cultivation, and go a-begging for their bare livelihood. We must not imagine that we are one of these disinherited peoples of the world. The time has come for us to break open the treasure trove of our ancestors and use it for our commerce of life. Let us, with its help, make our future our own – never continue our existence as the eternal rag-picker at other people's dustbins.[7]

Tagore's own way forward in the entire debate on the role and relevance of culture in our national life was the basing of our own structure on "a synthesis of all the different cultures that we have".[8] When taking a stand in such a centre, Tagore argued:

> Our gaze shall no longer be timid and dazed; our heads shall remain erect, safe from insult. For then we shall be able to take our own views of the Truth, from the standpoint of our own vantage ground, thus opening out a new vista of thought before the grateful world.[9]

It was essential for him that our cultural past be rediscovered, revivified and be used to "make our future our own".

Some of the leading thought-leaders of the early nationalist period in India actively participated in and developed a discourse on Indian culture. Apart from trying to define the

---

[7] Rabindranath Tagore, "The Centre of Indian Culture", in S.K. Das, ed., *The English Writings of Rabindranath Tagore (EWRT)*, vol. 2, 2008, p. 487.

[8] Ibid., p. 485.

[9] Ibid.

essentials of culture from the ethical and philosophical point of view, these thinkers – in developing the cultural discourse – vigorously took on the colonialist perceptions and interpretations of Indian culture by trying to develop Indian paradigms to its study and understanding. Their actions had a robustly creative side and saw the launching of nationalist educational and cultural movements as well as the creation of nationalist institutions in order to support and perpetuate these efforts. The National Education Movement, the creation of the National College in Calcutta and the growth of the nationalist art movement were some of the manifestations of this rich cultural quest. It was an epoch when the nationalist cultural discourse was sought to be developed as a supplementing pillar of the nationalist political effort. The entire debate and its expressions were remarkable for their breadth, variety and freedom. There was an unhesitating discussion on culture, its role and necessity in the larger movement of Indian nationalism. Cultural nationalism seems to have been seen and accepted by a number of thinkers then as a legitimate instrument for pursuing the goal of Indian freedom.

It appeared to me that it would be interesting to take a look at some of the facets of this discourse on Indian culture that gradually evolved during this early period. I found it equally interesting to discover the concerns of some of our founding fathers, during a later phase, for the rediscovery of cultural India. It intrigued me to see how they sought to give this quest a certain primacy in their national life and how they hoped to use it as an instrument for reinventing and advancing India's ties with countries in her neighbouring region. They seem to have clearly felt that in India's multidirectional march towards development, the cultural field had to also be taken into consideration, and newer methods and frameworks needed to be evolved in order to generate and sustain a renewed cultural outlook, consciousness and activism.

This work, then, looks at the dimensions of this debate on Indian culture and attempts to revisit some of the leading minds of the epoch – cultural nationalists – who had set the parameters of the cultural debate and imparted to it a varied dimension, perspective and hue. I have started with examining Swami Vivekananda's interest in Indian and world cultures and gone on to read from some of the leading cultural nationalists of the early nationalist period. A reading of Sister Nivedita and John Woodroffe reveals how culture and its national role in India became central to those Westerners who, adopting the Indian way of life, Hinduized themselves completely. Ananda Coomaraswamy, Sister Nivedita and Sri Aurobindo formed the famed cultural nationalist triad of the age. Each with their forceful cultural writings as well as activism injected new dynamism to the debate. They preceded other Indian leaders at least by a decade in their assessment that the nationalist political movement needed to be infused with a cultural dimension and debate, they saw this as one of the lasting contributions of the age. Interestingly some of their writings on the issue remain strikingly relevant today in the context of globalization and the homogenization as well as the asymmetries of cultures. I found it interesting thus, to weave in a reading of the triad.

Syama Prasad Mookerjee and K.M. Munshi have also found place in my reading of Indian cultural nationalists. Mookerjee's brief foray in South-East Asia as a cultural ambassador for India and his firm belief, in the early years of Independence, that India should seriously look to rebuild her civilizational bridges with the people and countries of the region are little known today. Munshi's contribution towards popularizing India's languages and her culture is hardly discussed today and his role as an integrator of cultures remains ignored. Towards the end I have discussed some of Jawaharlal

Nehru's observations on the handling of culture and cultural institutions in newly-independent India. Nehru was not a cultural nationalist in the mould of the early thinkers. While the political and cultural movement was ripening at home he was but a callow student in faraway Harrow faced with a medley of "conflicting desires" that cast a shadow of vagueness and confusion over his understanding of the movement back home.[10] I have often wondered whether Nehru understood at all the early Indian cultural nationalists and whether he could really comprehend the magnitude of their contribution to the national movement which he was to lead in the later years. However, I have included him primarily because as Prime Minister, Nehru did display an interest in the use of culture for national development. Whether he really took forward this interest through effective cultural manifestations and expressions is a matter that remains open to debate. Nevertheless by referring to the need for cultural awareness in the country Nehru did impart to the issue some space in the discourse on national development and growth.

The work also briefly looks at the present state of apathy and neglect of culture in our national scheme of development and pleads for an urgent remedying of this habit and trend. It calls for a renewal of that vigorous and multidimensional debate on Indian culture which had dominated the early decades of the last century and argues for a revisiting and a re-examining of the deeper fundamentals and principals of that debate. It also argues for a renewed effort to bring to the centrestage the debate on Indian culture at a time when its moorings seem to be loosening and its symbols diluting. In a sense, it's a case for the recognition of Indian culture in India!

---

[10] Jawaharlal Nehru, *Toward Freedom*, 1941, p. 34.

Part I

1

Vivekananda
A "Fascination" with Culture

LET us begin our journey in trying to unravel facets of the debate on culture in India by looking at the thoughts of one who did much in his time to establish interest in India on the world stage. His intervention, often seen as a watershed event, helped give a new turn to the study and to the perception of India and also awakened in a large number of Indians the urge to study India, Indian culture, Indian history, and to try and present to the world a distinctly Indian point of view. Swami Vivekananda was indeed a dynamic cultural ambassador of Indian civilization apart from being one of the principal standard bearers of Indian spiritual thought and vision.

In the years when it was fashionable to study Indian art and culture through the Hellenic prism and the habit of trying to establish an overwhelming foreign influence on Indian culture dominated, Vivekananda was one of those early trend-setters who sought to reverse the gaze.[1] It is as a great cultural enthusiast and connoisseur that Vivekananda travelled in India and the world. His works are replete with allusions to the culture and civilizations of the world and to the culture of India. Through a ceaseless focus on culture Vivekananda seemed to have given a certain centrality to the issue of culture in India. At a time when colonial domination at all levels of Indian life was total

---

[1] Sankari Prasad Basu, *Nivedita Lokmata*, vol. 4, BENG 1401, p. 21.

Vivekananda's discussion of Indian culture seemed to have created a stir among his listeners and adherents. Let us read of some of this and know of his concern for the fundamentals of India's culture. His travels and conversations provide some of the best insights into his active interest in the culture of his land and of other lands as well.

In his *parivrajak* (wandering monk) days Vivekananda observed and absorbed with great attention and depth representations of Indian architecture, art and painting.[2] Narratives of his itinerant days in northern India describe his fascination with Indian art and culture. While traversing Lucknow he admired the grandeur of the city's gardens and palaces and in Agra, he is said to have visited the Taj Mahal "many times, seeing it from different angles". Referring to the Taj, Vivekananda once remarked:

> Every square inch of this wondrous edifice is worth a whole day's patient observation, and it requires at least six months to make a real study of it.[3]

In April 1891, during his peregrinations, Vivekananda visited the celebrated Dilwara Temples in the province of Rajaputana. Built by the Chalukyas between the eleventh and thirteenth centuries CE, these temples were the best examples of exquisite Indian marble architecture and the Swami "spent days examining [their] glories".[4]

---

2 Sankari Prasad Basu, *Nivedita Lokmata*, vol. 4, p. 22.

3 *The Life of Swami Vivekananda by His Eastern and Western Disciples* (henceforth *The Life*), vol. 1, 6th edn., 1998, p. 217. While visiting the Taj, he had movingly remarked that, "If you squeeze a bit of this marble, it will drip drops of royal love and its sorrow." It was in the context of studying the Taj's "interior works of beauty" that he had said that such an effort would require at least six months of study. (*The Complete Works of Swami Vivekananda* (*CWSV*), vol. 5, p. 421.)

4 *The Life*, vol. 1, p. 279.

fig. 1: Dilwara Group of Temples in Mount Abu, 1865
Courtesy: British Library Online Gallery

Those who came in contact with Vivekananda during this phase and even later, recalled his enthusiasm and deft capacity to discuss art, Indian and Western; each day he would enthrall groups with new areas of knowledge. He would "descant on the idealization of the sensuous in Greek art, and then would go on to contrast it with the whole trend of Hindu art and culture towards the supersensuous".[5] In every discussion on art and culture, the Swami sought to open the eyes of his young adherents to the physical manifestations of what was an essentially spiritual vision. His studies of Indian architecture led him into the spirit of Indian culture and its unique style of manifestation and expression. In a conversation with a young adherent, Priyanath Sinha, who left us records of the Swami's lively interest in Indian culture, he once spoke of the distinct style and ethos of Indian architecture:

5 *The Life*, vol. 1, p. 365.

> People say Calcutta is a city of palaces, but the houses look much like so many boxes placed one upon the other! They convey no idea whatever. In Rajputana you can still find much pure Hindu architecture. If you look at a Dharmashala, you will feel as if it calls you with open arms to take shelter within and partake of its unqualified hospitableness. If you look at a temple, you are sure to find a Divine Presence in and about it. If you look about a rural cottage, you will at once be able to comprehend the special meanings of its different portions, and that the whole structure bears evidence to the predominant nature and ideal of the owner thereof.[6]

While outside India, Vivekananda continued with this inclination of his. In Sri Lanka, for example, he is said to have studied with great interest Sinhalese art at Anuradhapura and other cities of the country.[7] Everywhere that he went, Vivekananda not only saw the cultural and artistic manifestations of various civilizations but also tried to rediscover and establish their links with India's culture and civilization. Wherever he perceived India's reach, her cultural and spiritual presence, he seemed fascinated and captivated. Visits to museums and other cultural repositories engrossed him for hours together. While in Singapore he described various things that caught his attention but did not fail to mention that the city "possesses a fine museum too".[8]

---

6 *CWSV*, vol. 5, pp. 421-22.

7 Basu, op. cit., p. 22. In his first journey westward in 1893 Vivekananda described to his Madras disciples his journey in South-East Asia. In a letter written from the "Oriental Hotel, Yokohama", and dated 10 July 1893, the Swami mentioned the near day-long halt at Colombo and how he "took the opportunity of getting off to have a look at the town". What struck him "was a temple in which was a very gigantic *Murti* (image) of the Lord Buddha in a reclining posture, entering *Nirvâna*". (*CWSV*, vol. 5, p. 6.)

8 *CWSV*, vol. 5, p. 6.

fig. 2: The statues "beautifully carved out of wood" of "500 first disciples of Buddha", inside the temple at Canton as Vivekananda must have seen them. Photo c. 1900/Photo courtesy: https://khnemo.files. wordpress.com

During his first Westward journey, while his ship anchored at Hong Kong for three days, the Swami visited Canton. Here too he marvelled at India's cultural imprints.

> I went to see several Chinese temples. The biggest in Canton is dedicated to the memory of the first Buddhistic Emperor and the 500 first disciples of Buddhism. The central figure is of course of Buddha, and next beneath Him is seated the Emperor, and ranging on both sides are the statues of the disciples, all beautifully carved out of wood.[9]

Studying the "ancient Buddhist carvings" and wondering "at the artistry of the wooden images" the jubilant monk noted the "points of similarity and dissimilarity between Buddhist and Indian temples" and is said to have "delighted in the originality that he found" there.[10]

---

9 *CWSV*, vol. 5, p. 8.

10 *The Life*, vol. 1, p. 395. A perennial student and exponent of comparative civilizational studies, Vivekananda noted that in "more isolated portions of the building he was shown many Sanskrit manuscripts, written, strange to say, in old Bengali characters". (Ibid., p. 397.)

In the same trip, the Swami transited through Japan. As he wrote, after seeing Nagasaki and from thence to Kobe he "gave up the steamer and took the land-route to Yokohama, with a view to see the interior of Japan". Here too he was attracted by the many facets of Japanese life and society, including the cultural. "I saw quite a lot of temples," he wrote in the same letter, "in every temple there are some Sanskrit *Mantra*s written in old Bengali characters".[11]

Whether it was America or Europe, wherever he went, Vivekananda visited museums and marvelled at their art and artefact collections. Nor was he simply an observer of cultures, he had studied them in his own way and became an exponent of the study of world cultures.[12] During his second visit to the West, the *Los Angeles Times* of 21 January 1900 gave an interesting report of his speech at the Shakespeare Club:

> Swami Vivekananda gave an exceedingly interesting lecture on Persian art, dwelling particularly on the architecture, the decorative art, the manufacture of shawls and carpets by the Persians, and also speaking of the philosophy of art.[13]

In fact, the reporter of the *Los Angeles Herald* thought he was actually listening to a Persian and wrote:

---

11 *CWSV*, vol. 5, p. 9.

12 In a letter written to Mary Hale, in 1897 Vivekananda made a number of interesting observations based on his reading of Indian art and his visits to the centres of the world's culture and civilization. Referring to his visit to Rome, he wrote "I enjoyed Rome more than anything in the West, and after seeing Pompeii I have lost all regard for the so-called 'Modern Civilisation'. With the exception of steam and electricity they had everything else and infinitely more art conceptions and executions than the Moderns." (*CWSV*, vol. 8, p. 395.)

13 Marie Louis Burke, *Swami Vivekananda in the West: New Discoveries* (henceforth *In the West*), vol. 5, 4th ed., 1998, p. 274.

> The reception was tendered to the Swami Vivekananda. There were music and recitations, and then the guest of the occasion delivered a lecture upon the Persian art of making rugs, carpets, shawls and in decorations of the kinds in which the natives of Persia excel. The lecture was highly instructive to those interested in these things. . . . The Persian was engaged [?] to deliver a series of lectures on kindred subjects during the week beginning on Monday. . . .[14]

In Paris, it was his "cherished desire to remain for some time and study the French language and civilization".[15] He himself recounted that it was from his visits to the Musée de Louvre that he "came to understand the three stages of Greek art".[16] And in his memoirs of his European travel the Swami detailed these stages as he learnt them from these visits. His descriptions of the artistic expressions of these stages easily demonstrate the depth with which he seemed to have studied them.

His travelling companions, all Westerners and some of them famous and established in their own fields, such as the legendary French Soprano Emma Calvé (1858–1942), remembered how the Swami acted as the real guide and teacher during these excursions. Jospehine Macleod recalled how the few days in Vienna in October 1900 were spent for the most part in "sight-seeing going through the Schönbrunn Palace, the Museum, the Art Gallery. . . ."[17] To travel with the Swami was "an education in itself". While visiting these sites

---

14 *In the West*, vol. 5, pp. 274-75.

15 *CWSV*, vol. 7, pp. 372-73. He saw Paris as the "fountain-head of European civilization, as Gomukhi is of the Ganga" and pointed out that the "sculptor, the painter, the musician, the dancer, or any artist, if he can first obtain celebrity in Paris, acquires very easily the esteem and eulogy of other countries." (*CWSV*, vol. 5, pp. 510-11.)

16 *CWSV*, vol. 7, p. 402.

17 *In the West*, vol. 6, p. 385.

in the city he began a detailed analysis of European politics and history:

> The Schönbrunn Palace, for instance, put him in mind of the whole pageant of Austrian history – its powerful, prestigious, and glamorous past, its declining present, and its probable eclipse in the future.[18]

In every historic city that he went, even if it be for a short while, the museum seemed to have attracted Vivekananda most. In the same trip, while in Istanbul, he described his visit to the museum which was "situated where the ancient harem of the Greek Emperors once stood" and noted the "remarkable sarcophagi and other things".[19]

The visit to Greece, during this phase seemed to have equally excited him; from Port Piraeus (near Athens) the party drove "five miles to have a look at the ancient walls of Athens which used to connect the city with the port". Then, recounts Vivekananda in some detail, his exposure to the ancient Hellenic art, culture and religion:

> We went through the town; the Acropolis, the hotels, houses. . . . The palace is a small one. The same day, again, we climbed the hillock and had a view of the Acropolis, the temple of the Wingless Victory, and the Parthenon, etc. The temple is made of white marble. Some standing remains of columns also we saw. The next day we again went to see these. . . . On the second day we visited the temple of Olympian Zeus, Theatre Dionysius etc., as far as the sea-shore. The third day we set out for Eleusis, which was the chief religious seat of the Greeks. Here it was that the famous Eleusinian Mysteries used to be played.[20]

---

18 *In the west*, vol. 6, p. 386.

19 *CWSV*, vol. 7, p. 399.

20 *CWSV*, vol. 7, p. 401. The standard tourist guide-book of the period, *Greece: Handbook for Travellers*, that appeared in 1894, under the Karl →

Calvé has left behind a vivid description of the Swami and his ways in these cradles of world culture and civilization. She movingly recalled:

> With the swami and some of his friends and followers I went upon a most remarkable trip, through Turkey, Egypt and Greece. . . . What a pilgrimage it was! Science, philosophy and history had no secrets from the swami. I listened with all my ears to the wise and learned discourse that went on around me. . . . When we were in Greece we visited Eleusis. He explained its mysteries to us and led us from altar to altar, from temple to temple, describing the processions that were held in each place, intoning the ancient prayers, showing us the priestly rites. Later, in Egypt, one unforgettable night, he led us again into the past, speaking to us in mystic, moving words, under the shadow of the silent Sphinx.[21]

It is interesting to note that Vivekananda would often engage in archaeological and historical discussions but – as one of his leading chroniclers, the historian Sankari Prasad Basu notes –

→ Baedeker imprint, describes Eleusis as a "poor fever-haunted village, with 1200 inhabitants. . . . The widespread celebrity of its name is derived from the worship of Demeter, the 'Eleusinian Mysteries' of which, believed to symbolize the highest and holiest feelings of mankind, continued to be solemnly celebrated down to the end of the fourth century of the present era." (Karl Baedeker, *Greece: Handbook for Travellers*, 1894, pp. 115-17.) The Swami and his party might have referred to copies of the popular handbook during their travels!

21 *In the West*, vol. 6, p. 395. Also see Emma Calvé, *My Life* (trans. Rosamond Gilder), 1922, pp. 188-91. Swami Vidyatmananda, *Vivekananda in Europe*, 2012, p. 271. J.P. Mahaffy (1839–1919) "classicist and polymath" in his celebrated *Rambles and Studies in Greece* written eight years before Vivekananda's visit, referred to Eleusis, to the Eleusinian mysteries and described the ruins as he saw them. It gives an idea of the ruins as Vivekananda must have seen them. "The wretched modern village of Eleusis is picturesquely situated near the →

most of these have been lost because there was no one in the group who seriously noted these down for posterity.[22] Apart from Nivedita, it is Calvé who gave glimpses of this very interesting but less discussed aspect of the Swami's personality. While in Greece, Vivekananda also visited the national museum and Calvé noted:

> The Museum contains the most beautiful collection of amphores in the world. I saw the delicious statue of Minerva Athena. . . . That bizarre girdle formed of two snakes, their heads raised. The serpent, the Swami tells us, is found again and again in all religions: the Virgin Mary crushing the serpent, the archangel Michael squashing the dragon – the most ancient civilizations known to man adore the serpent – the emblem of wisdom, of prudence, of force: Moses, the Hindus, the Egyptians and Christianity. The word "mage" [magician] – "gatur" – [probably "jadu"] in Hindu – means "charm", "charmer", "master of the serpent" – that is to say, master in God; this word "mage" comes from that same adoration of serpents.[23]

→ sea, on the old site, and there are still to be seen the ruins." Mahaffy found the ruins "defaced" and all that was visible were "vast fragments of pillars and capitals, and a great pavement, all of white marble, along which the ancient wheel-tracks are distinctly visible". Referring to the "Mysteries", which were now lost "beyond recall" he noted, "It is . . . the celebrated Mysteries – the *Great Eleusinia*, as they were called – which give to the village of Eleusis, with its hopeless ruins, so deep an interest. . . ." (*Rambles and Studies in Greece*, 1892, pp. 207-13.)

[22] Sankari Prasad Basu, *Vivekananda O Samakālin Bhāratbarsha* (Vivekananda and Contemporary India), vol. 5, 6th imp. 2009, p. 299. Basu devotes a whole volume to discussing Vivekananda's interest in and contribution to Indian culture, literature and art and gives copious references to the Swami's discussion on these topics. I have greatly benefited from his work while discussing Vivekananda's position and role in debating culture.

[23] *Vivekananda in Europe*, pp. 267-68, *Samakālin Bhāratbarṣa*, pp. 299-300.

fig. 3: Eleusis — seat of the famous "Eleusinian Mysteries"
Courtesy: http://www.abu.nb.ca/

One of Vivekananda's chief disciples, Sister Nivedita – of whose participation in debating Indian culture we shall read in some detail in a later section – also witnessed Vivekananda's cultural, archaeological and artistic eye during her wandering with him in the Himalayas. In her *Notes on the Wanderings with the Swami Vivekananda*, Nivedita recounts how Vivekananda gave them archaeological lessons in studying Indian temple architecture. Nivedita's description of the temple itself reflects her own quite detailed observation and study of Indian temple architecture:

> . . . in a wood by the side of the Jhelum, we discovered the long-sought Temple of Pandrenthan (Pandresthan, place of the Pandavas?). It was sunk in a pond, and this was thickly covered with scum, out of which it rose, a tiny cathedral of long ago, built of heavy grey limestone. The temple consisted of a small cell, with four doorways, opening to the cardinal points. Externally, it was a tapering pyramid – with its top truncated, to give foothold to a bush – supported on a four-pierced pedestal. In its architecture, trefoil and triangular arches were combined, in an unusual fashion, with each other, and with the straight line lintel. It was built with marvellous solidity, and the necessary lines were somewhat obscured by heavy ornament.[24]

Once there, the members of the party were given their first archaeological lessons by the Swami himself. As Nivedita recalled the moment:

> For all but the Swami himself, this was our first peep at Indian Archaeology. So when he had been through it, he taught us how to observe the interior. In the centre of the ceiling was a large sun-medallion, set in a square whose points were the points of the compass. This left four equal triangles, at the corners of the ceiling, which were filled with sculpture in low relief, male and female figures intertwined with serpents, beautifully done. On the wall were empty spaces, where seemed to have been a band of topes.
>
> Outside, carvings were similarly distributed. In one of the trefoil arches – over, I think, the eastern door – was a fine image of the Teaching Buddha, standing, with His hand uplifted. Running round the buttresses was a much defaced frieze of a seated woman, with a tree – evidently Mâyâ Devi, the Mother of Buddha. The three other door-niches were empty. . . . The masonry of this little temple was superb, and probably accounted for its long preservation. A single block

[24] Sister Nivedita, *Notes of Some Wandering with the Swami Vivekananda*, 1913, p. 113.

> of stone would be so cut as to correspond, not to one brick in a wall, but to a section of the architect's plan. It would turn a corner and form part of two distinct walls, or sometimes even of three. . . . The theory of the workmen seemed so much more that of carpentering than of building! The water about it, was probably an overflow, into the temple-court, from the sacred spring that the chapel itself may have been placed, as the Swami thought, to enshrine.[25]

To the Swami, the place was "delightfully suggestive. It was a direct memorial of Buddhism, representing one of the four religious periods into which he had already divided the history of Kashmir:

1. Tree and Snake-worship, from which dated all the names of the springs ending in Nâg, such as Vêrnâg, and so on;
2. Buddhism;
3. Hinduism, in the form of Sun-worship; and
4. Mohammedanism.

Sculpture, he told us, was the characteristic art of Buddhism, and the sun-medallion, or lotus, one of its commonest ornaments. The figures with the serpents referred to pre-Buddhism."[26]

While trying to describe Vivekananda's awareness of and interest in Indian culture and its various manifestations, the above description by Nivedita gives an insight into what Vivekananda taught them to discern while trying to study specimens of Indian art and temple architecture.

It was during the same wandering that Nivedita saw the Swami explaining another important aspect of Indian culture,

---

[25] Sister Nivedita, *Notes of Some Wandering with the Swami Vivekananda*, 1913, pp. 114-16.

[26] Ibid., pp. 116-17.

fig. 4: The temple at Pandrenathan as it stands today
Courtesy: Shri Chander M. Bhat

worship and nature. It was on 29 June 1898, as Nivedita narrated, that the party visited the "Takt-i-Suleimân, a little temple very massively built, on the summit of a small mountain 2,000 or 3,000 ft high".[27] Nivedita found it "beautiful and peaceful" and was attracted by the sight of the "Floating Gardens" below for miles around. Here too the Swami began animatedly explaining one of his positions:

> The Takt-i-Suleimân was one of the great illustrations of the Swami's argument, when he would take up the subject of the Hindu love of Nature as shown in the choice of sites for temples and architectural monuments. As he had declared, in London, that the saints lived on the hill-tops, in order to enjoy the scenery, so now he pointed out – citing one example after another – that our Indian people always

[27] Sister Nivedita, *Notes of Some Wandering with the Swami Vivekananda*, 1913, p. 97.

consecrated places of peculiar beauty and importance, by making there their altars of worship. And there was no denying that the little Takt, crowning the hill that dominated the whole valley, was a case in point.[28]

fig. 5: Martand Temple, *c*. 1900.
Courtesy: http://www.oldindianphotos

Nivedita witnessed a similar scene of great interest when the party visited the ancient Martand Temple dedicated to the sun near Srinagar. The Swami "was hard at work, in an instant, on observations and theories, pointing out the cornice that ran along the nave from the entrance to the sanctuary, to the west, surmounted by the high trefoils of the two arches and also by a freize; or showing us the panel containing cherubs. . . ."[29] Not

---

28 Sister Nivedita, *Notes of Some Wandering with the Swami Vivekananda*, 1913, pp. 97-98.

29 Sister Nivedita, *Notes of Some Wandering with the Swami Vivekananda*, 1913, p. 137.

one occasion such as these did he let go by without a lesson in Indian culture and architecture.

Vivekananda encouraged his Western disciples to make first-hand studies of Indian art and architecture. Till his last days he was concerned that a true understanding and appreciation of Indian art and culture develop, not only among Indians, but also permeate the thoughts of the Western scholar and seeker. He expressed happiness at the celebrated actress Sarah Bernhardt's (1844–1923) appreciation of India and at her efforts of trying to spread an authentic idea of India. In his memoirs the Swami noted:

> Madame Bernhardt has a special regard for India; she tells me again and again that our country is "*très ancien, très civilisé*" – very ancient and very civilized. One year she performed a drama touching on India, in which she set up a whole Indian street-scene on the stage – men, women, and children, *sadhu*s, *naga*s, and everything – an exact picture of India! After the performance she told me that for about a month she had visited every museum and made herself acquainted with the men and women and their dress, the streets and bathing *ghat*s and every thing relating to India. Madame Bernhardt has a very strong desire to visit India – "*C'est mon rêve*! – it is the dream of my life", she says.[30]

In a letter dated 10 February 1902, about five months before his passing away one reads his suggestions and directions to Mrs Ole Bull and Nivedita, who had just returned from a Western trip:

> I wish it so much that you should go for a few hours to a few villages west of Calcutta to see the old Bengali structures made of wood, bamboo, cane, mica, and grass. These are the bungalows, most artistic. Alas! the name is travested nowadays by every pigsty appropriating the name. In old

30 *CWSV*, vol. 7, p. 374.

> days a man who built a palace still built a bungalow for the reception of guests. The art is dying out. I wish I could build the whole of Nivedita's School in that style. Yet it is good to see the few that yet remain, at least one.[31]

Vivekananda's spiritually active and intellectually restless mind was forever comparing cultures, civilizations and arts. Ceaselessly did he investigate the sources of various arts, their deeper motivating spirit and ideal, and wherever he could he described his quest. For a while he was also involved in examining Indian art and whether there was on it any overweening Greek, read Western influence. It was, as we shall later see, one of the debates of the age and Vivekananda participated in it speaking for Indian culture. He expounded

---

31 *Letters of Swami Vivekananda*, 16th imp., 2007, p. 453. Referring to this decline of the Indian architectural style a few years after the Swami's comment, Coomaraswamy too lamented its gradual demise. Derisively pointing at the vulgarization of modern Indian architecture which failed to reflect the spirit of Indian culture and put out of work a large number of traditional Indian craftsmen, Coomaraswamy wrote, ". . . The creative force in us has died, because we had no faith in ourselves – we could only learn to be intellectual parasites; to make . . . of our country a mere suburb of Birmingham and Paris." In many parts of India, he witnessed the "very fine tradition of building" still surviving but gradually "being killed by neglect". While the modern Indian architecture, "however domestic or palatial" was "at the very lowest ebb [and] the average modern house [was] a cross between a suburban villa and a Government barrack". Coomaraswamy accused the "Swadeshist politician" of not addressing this issue, it did not occur to any of them to "demand from the Government that in public buildings Indian architecture" be made the rule and "Indian architects employed or that the State" patronise and "foster Indian artistic industries". Everywhere in the country there are still living a large number of "hereditary and most capable working architects – such as no other country in the world still possesses – but like other craftsmen they are being starved by neglect and forced to adopt menial or agricultural work for a bare living" commented Coomaraswamy. (*Art and Swadeshi*, pp. 12-16.)

once on Greek and Indian art, it must have been a sight to see him animatedly speak on the subject:

> The secret of Greek Art is its imitation of nature even to the minutest details; whereas the secret of Indian Art is to represent the ideal . . . true Art can be compared to a lily which springs from the ground, takes its nourishment from the ground, and yet is quite high above it. So Art must be in touch with nature – and wherever that touch is gone, Art degenerates – yet it must be above nature. Art is – representing the beautiful. There must be Art in everything. The difference between architecture and building is that the former expresses an idea, while the latter is merely a structure built on economic principles. The value of matter depends solely on its capacities of expressing *ideas*.
>
> The artistic faculty was highly developed in our Lord, Shri Ramakrishna, and he used to say that without this faculty none can be truly spiritual.[32]

The nationalist in Vivekananda asserted itself when it came to interpreting and presenting Indian culture and he hoped that the West would, in a true spirit, discover the fundamentals of that culture. The internationalist in him continuously advocated the need for India to reach out to the world, to be part of its growth and modern progress and to absorb from its multitudes of culture and artistic manifestations.[33] In the letter from Yokohama, Vivekananda exhorted his young adherents to go out and see the world,

---

32 *CWSV*, vol. 5, pp. 258-59.

33 In a letter, written to one of his chief Western disciples in 1897, while returning from his first tour to the West, the Swami displayed this internationalism, this spirit of a global citizen within himself, "From Suez begins Asia. Once more Asia. What am I? Asiatic, European, or American? I feel a curious medley of personalities in me." (*CWSV*, vol. 8, p. 395.)

> Come out of your narrow holes and have a look abroad. See how nations are on the march![34]

A number of Indian cultural nationalists, who followed Vivekananda, had similar nationalist and internationalist perceptions. He articulated this again in a letter to one of his disciples:

> Keeping aloof from the community of nations is the only cause for the downfall of India. . . . Everyone that comes out of the country confers a benefit on the whole nation; for it is by doing that alone that your horizon will expand. . . . All narrowness, all contraction, all selfishness is simply slow suicide, and when a nation commits the fatal mistake of contracting itself and of thus cutting off all expansion and life, it must die.[35]

As he encouraged this going out into the world Vivekananda also encouraged those who wished to come to India, aspired to study her culture and life and evolve a new assessment of her traditions and message. Nivedita noted the "passionate enthusiasm" with which Vivekananda introduced India, her life and culture to his Western disciples during their journey with him in northern India in 1898:

> What scenes were those through which we journeyed from the beginning of May until the end of October! And with what passionate enthusiasm were we introduced one by one to each point of interest, as we reached it! The ignorance of educated Western people about India – excepting of course those who have in some measure specialized on the subject – might almost be described as illiteracy, and our object-lessons began . . . with Patna, the ancient Pataliputra, itself. The river-front of Benares, as one approaches it by railway

---

[34] *CWSV*, vol. 5, p. 10.

[35] Letter to Manmathanath Bhattacharya, 5 September 1894 in *The Life*, p. 554.

> from the East, is amongst the sights of the world, and could not fail of our leader's eager praise.[36]

But it was not Vivekananda's habit to rest content by simply imparting the broad picture of Indian life and culture to his disciples. He was at his best when he dwelt on the details and described their essence. This aspect may not be linked to culture alone, but the Swami's ways of disseminating knowledge and understanding of India was by itself a wide education of culture. Nivedita's description of this aspect seems to by far surpass others:

> . . . it was not only the great cities of admitted beauty and historic importance, that the Swami, in his eagerness, would strive to impress on our memory. Perhaps nowhere did his love seem more ardent, or his absorption more intense, than as we passed across the long stretches of the Plains, covered with fields and farms and villages. Here his thought was free to brood over the land as a whole, and he would spend hours explaining the communal system of agriculture, or describing the daily life of the farm housewife. . . .[37]

Vivekananda displayed a remarkably developed "historic consciousness", that impelled him to espouse the cause of his country's culture and history, which, he felt, had to be reassessed and restated. Observed Nivedita:

> It would seem sometimes as if the Swami lived and moved and had his very being in the sense of his country's past. His historic consciousness was extraordinarily developed. Thus, as we journeyed across the Terai, in the hot hours of an afternoon near the beginning of the rains, we were made to feel that this was the very earth on which had passed the youth and renunciation of Buddha. The wild peacocks spoke to us of Rajputana and her ballad lore. An occasional

---

[36] Sister Nivedita, *The Master as I Saw Him*, 1910, p. 114.

[37] Ibid., p. 115.

> elephant was the text for tales of ancient battles, and the story of an India that was never defeated so long as she could oppose to the tide of conquest the military walls of these living artillery.[38]

Vivekananda showed a similar enthusiasm when the Japanese artist and art historian Okakura Kakuzo (1862–1913) came to India to visit the principal centres of Indian art and culture. He saw in the visit an opportunity to renew his ties with Japan, a country that he loved, and also an occasion to create a greater Asian solidarity through the cultural and spiritual link. He planned the entire cultural itinerary of his Japanese guest and despite failing health agreed to accompany Okakura to Bodh-Gaya and spent days studying the area and explaining its artistic and cultural significance.[39] One of his young disciples, Naresh Chandra Ghosh, who had accompanied Vivekananda during this trip recalled how the Master, during their over a week's stay at Bodh-Gaya, would frequent the temple everyday and explain to them in great detail its art and symbolism.[40] While at Benares during this period he is said to have everyday held discussions on Indian art, music and

---

38 *The Master as I Saw Him*, pp. 116-17.

39 Nivedita in her classic representation of her Master, while discussing his attitude to the Buddha recalled that during the Master's "boyhood" the country's attention had been riveted on the "story of Buddhism" because of the restoration work undertaken at Bodh-Gaya during that period. The archaeologist Rajendralal Mitra was one of the chief supervisors of this entire project. Nivedita noted that Vivekananda undertook an assiduous study of Buddhism and while at it studied in detail Rajendralal's opus "Buddha-Gaya: The Hermitage of Sakya Muni". Swami Akhandananda in his reminiscences of Vivekananda also remembered seeing the young Narendranath studying Mitra's volume on the Bodh-Gaya. *The Master as I Saw Him*, pp. 324-26; *Samakālin Bhāratbarṣa*, p. 92.)

40 *Nivedita Lokmata*, p. 42.

drama. Those listening could not but marvel at his versatility in expounding these.[41]

The Swami closely followed Okakura's cultural tour and in his letter of 10th February 1902, expressed his deep concern for reviving the arts of India and for arresting their steady decline. It is worth quoting the rest of the letter:

> Mr. Okakura has started on his short tour. He intends to visit Agra, Gwalior, Ajanta, Ellora, Chittore, Udaipur, Jaipur and Delhi. A very well-educated rich young man of Varanasi, with whose father we had a long-standing friendship, came back to this city yesterday. He is especially interested in art, and spending purposely a lot of money in his attempts to revive dying Indian arts. He came to see me only a few hours after Mr. Okakura left. He is just the man to show him artistic India (i.e. what little is left), and I am sure he will be much benefited by Okakura's suggestions. Okakura just found a common terracotta water-vessel here used by the servants. The shape and the embossed work on it simply charmed him, but as it is common earthenware and would not bear the journey he left a request with me to have it reproduced in brass. I was at my wit's end as to what to do. My young friend comes a few hours after, and not only undertakes to have it done but offers to show a few hundreds of embossed designs in terracotta infinitely superior to the one Okakura fancied.
>
> He also offers to show us old paintings in that wonderful old style. Only one family is left in Varanasi who can paint after the old style yet. One of them has painted a whole hunting scene on a pea, perfect in detail and action. I hope Okakura will come to this city on his return and be this gentleman's guest and see a bit of what is left.[42]

---

41 *Nivedita Lokmata*, p. 43.

42 *CWSV*, vol. 5, pp. 174-75. A number of others, including Coomaraswamy, were disturbed at this rapid artistic degradation →

For Vivekananda the Indian ideal was "art", while the Western ideal he saw as "utility". The "Westerner looks for utility in everything, whereas with us art is everywhere. With the Western education, those beautiful *ghatis* [small water pots] of ours have been discarded, and enamel glasses have usurped their place in our homes!" What was needed was the "combination of art and utility". Japan, he pointed out, had done that quite early and had thus advanced rapidly.[43]

In his appraisal of Indian culture, what touched Vivekananda most was its capacity to "fascinate", as he movingly put it, in the mould of a true cultural messenger and interpreter of Indian culture:

> If there is one word in the English language to represent the gift of India to the world, if there is one word in the English language to express the effect which the literature of India produces upon mankind, it is this one word "fascination". It is the opposite of anything that takes you suddenly; it throws on you as it were, a charm imperceptibly. To many, Indian thought, Indian manners, Indian customs, Indian philosophy, Indian literature are repulsive at the first sight; but let them persevere, let them read, let them become familiar with the great principles underlying these ideas,

→ and disappearance. Highlighting the plight of the industrial arts in India and the decline of the traditional craftsmen, Coomaraswamy observed that such a disintegration was in the process not only in Benares, but "throughout India" where "the fine old art designs that [had] been attained after centuries of evolution [were] being abandoned and models utterly unsuited and far inferior artistically [were] being substituted". The famed Benares brass work, had by this time also degenerated, "they had departed from the fine old patterns that made Benares famous for its brass wares", most of them had turned into imitations of "European shapes and purposes". (*Art and Swadeshi*, pp. 17-19.)

43 Swami Vivekananda, "Indian Culture", in *The Vedanta Kesari*, vol. 88, December 2001, pp. 477-78.

> and it is ninety-nine to one that the charm will come over them, and fascination will be the result.[44]

Thus, Vivekananda, the "World-Teacher", the leonine exponent of the Vedanta, the one who gave a renewed voice to Hinduism on the world-stage, was equally a teacher of Indian culture, an exponent of its arts, heritage and values, as he was a teacher and student of world cultures. In making Indians and Westerners alike aware of India's culture and in encouraging Indians to seriously and independently engage in a study of their culture and art, Vivekananda played an important role. His expounding the Vedanta and the religions of India to the world was great, equally great was his effort at spreading the message and the essence of Indian culture. Vivekananda did set the tone, defined the path for the coming batches of cultural nationalists who were to take forward the debate on Indian culture. In a sense they were his cultural heirs.

---

44 Swami Vivekananda, "Indian Culture", in *The Vedanta Kesari*, vol. 88, December 2001, p. 476.

2

Ananda Coomaraswamy
A Case for Cultural Nationalism

ANANDA Kentish Coomaraswamy, one of the leading ideologues of the *swadeshi* epoch, essentially spoke of the need for Indian nationalism to concern itself with carrying forward the ideals of Indian culture from one age to another. Coomaraswamy also defined the perceptions of that culture by expanding and deepening it with the dimensions of the Indian ethico-spiritual thought. In his opuscule *Art and Swadeshi* written with the intention of imparting a cultural dimension to the nationalist movement then raging all over the country, Coomaraswamy tried to expand and define the very term culture. Admitting that it was one of those "harder" things to do, he wrote:

> . . . Plato identified it with the capacity for immediate and instinctive discrimination between good and bad workmanship, of whatever sorts; . . . We may expand this definition by including a certain quality of recollectedness or detachment, a capacity for stillness of mind and body (restlessness is essentially uncultured), and the power of penetrating mere externals in individual men or various races. Culture includes a view of life essentially balanced, where real and false values are not confused; also, I think, a certain knowledge of, or interest in, things which are not

> directly utilitarian, that is to say, which do not merely give pleasure to the senses or confirm a prejudice. . . .[1]

While defining the philosophical characteristics of culture, Coomaraswamy was also deeply concerned about the degradation of aesthetics that he saw all around – a dilution of the Indian mind's cultural approach and sensitivity. Interestingly, he did not spare the cultural artefacts of the *swadeshi* movement either and pointed out that these had not really taken off in trying to recreate the era of Indian aesthetic inspired by its past civilizational experience. He lamented:

> Modern India, Anglicized India, has produced no beauty and romance, but has gone far to destroy the beauty and romance which are our heritage from the past.[2]

In unusually strong words, Coomaraswamy observed that such was the magnitude of the fall that

> the modern amongst us can already tolerate an environment of cheap hideousness and tawdry, expensive discomfort, which would have disgusted the poorest in the days of Hindu or Mughal civilization.[3]

Enter a *swadeshi* shop, he pointed out and:

> You will not find the evidences of Indian invention, the wealth of beauty which the Indian craftsman used to lavish on the simplest articles of daily use, the filmy muslins or the flower-woven silks with which we used to worship the beauty of Indian women, the brazen vessels from which we ate and drank, the carpets on which we trod with bare feet. . . . You will not find these things, but you will find every kind of imitation of the productions of European commerce, differing

---

[1] Coomaraswamy, *Art and Swadeshi*, 1910, p. 25.

[2] Ibid., p. 2.

[3] Ibid., p. 18.

> only from their unlovely prototypes in their slightly higher price and slightly inferior quality. You will find dingy grey "shirtings"; other materials dyed with aniline dyes of the loudest and least permanent; travelling trunks that are painted every colour of the rainbow, and if carefully used may hold together for half a year; boot polish, marking ink, soaps and fountain pens – anything and everything but beauty. It is the outward sign of the merely material ideal of prosperity which is too exclusively striven for by our economists and politicians.[4]

This overshadowing of the Indian ideal of aesthetic by the "material ideal of prosperity" was what deeply troubled thought-leaders and cultural nationalists such as Coomaraswamy. "This loss of beauty in our lives," Coomaraswamy argued, "is a proof that we do not love India; for India, above all nations, was beautiful once, and that was not long ago".[5] The art historian was quite categorical that an India which had cast off her cultural and aesthetic ideal can never seriously seek to achieve a great power status. For him an "India, politically and economically free, but subdued by Europe in her inmost soul is scarcely an ideal to be dreamt of, or to live, or die, for." He saw India's "knowledge of beauty" as her unique contribution to humanity:

> "India, vulgarized by modern education, and by the ideals of modern commercialism, will never compensate humanity for India with its knowledge of beauty. . . ." Do you realize that when India was a great political power in Asia, when she colonized Java and inspired China, this also was the period of her greatest achievement in art? Has it never occurred to you that it is as much your duty to make your lives and your environment beautiful as to make them moral,

---

[4] Coomaraswamy, *Art and Swadeshi*, p. 2.

[5] Ibid., p. 4.

> in fact that without beauty there can be no true morality, without morality no true beauty?[6]

Coomaraswamy also lamented, what he termed, "the vulgarization of modern India" and argued that the "loss of the fine taste that belonged to classic and mediaeval culture [was] a sign of weakness, not of strength". He called upon all political nationalists of his period to "believe in the regeneration of India through art, and not by politics and economics alone".[7] A very crucial and relevant observation for present-day policy-makers and leaders to take note of!

Discerning as he was in matters of national education, Coomaraswamy saw the neglect of cultural education in the Indian system as responsible for the general apathy towards the study of Indian culture and art. His forthrightness in this matter was undisguized even when he spoke to an overwhelmingly foreign audience. An interesting instance of this was witnessed during a meeting of the Royal Society of Arts in London in January 1910 at which art critic and specialist of Indian art E.B. Havell (1861–1934) presented a paper on "Art Administration in India".[8] Coomaraswamy, seconding Havell's observations, added a lot more to the debate, he, in fact "thought Havell had said rather too little than too much of the apathy of the British government with regard to all matters connected with the Indian art". Anyone visiting for the first time the Indian section of the Museum at South Kensington, Coomaraswamy told his British audience, would come away without any

> special feeling of respect for, or any enlarged comprehension

---

[6] Coomaraswamy, *Art and Swadeshi*, p. 3.

[7] Ibid., pp. 3-4.

[8] Cited in S.P. Basu, *Nivedita Lokmata*, vol. 4, p. 128. Basu cites his source as the *Journal of the Royal Asiatic Society of Arts*, vol. LVIII, no. 985 (4 February 1910).

> of the expression of Indian thought and feeling in art. The museum was an emporium of industrial art, valuable as far as it went, than an effective record of an Indian creative imagination.[9]

This official callousness towards Indian art, Coomaraswamy reminded the professed art aficionados, also affected the Indian scene where large personal collections of Indian art were allowed to go to America – his own would one day be forced to relocate to the Boston Fine Arts Museum.[10] The same apathy percolated to Indian education, museums and art colleges:

> At the Bombay School of Art, where students might be

---

9 Basu, op. cit., p. 129. Coomaraswamy's observations on the India Museum were in fact universally felt at that time. The India Museum and its pattern of display were seen to be unmanageable. As Jonathan Jones art columnist for the *U.K. Guardian* observes, critics did complain that the India Museum was "crammed, claustrophobic and amateurish". *The Orientalist* in one of its issues complained of the conditions thus: "It is practically inaccessible, and hid away out of sight, and when you get to it you find a bonded warehouse and not a museum in straightforward airy order" (Jonathan Jones, "Art & Empire: The Forgotten Story of the India Museum", in *The Guardian*, 25 September 2003).

10 By 1916 Coomaraswamy had put together a large collection of "valuable classical Indian arts" especially "a series of miniature paintings with motifs of Hindu myths" and tried in vain to look for an academic job in the field of the study of Indian arts in India while proposing to donate his collection towards the setting up of a national museum of Indian art in Varanasi (Benares). The offer was rejected by the British Indian government. In 1917 Coomaraswamy was given an offer by Denman W. Ross (1853–1935) of Harvard University "to start and head the Indian Art Department at the Boston Museum of Fine Arts. In this way, Coomaraswamy and his arts collection moved to Boston – never to return to India" (see e.g. Rasoul Sorkhabi, "Ananda K. Coomaraswamy: From Geology to *Philosophia Perennis*", in *Current Science*, vol. 94, no. 3, 10 February 2008, p. 398).

> observed making shadings from antique casts and drawing of Gothic or pseudo-classic architecture, there was not a single good specimen of mediaeval Indian painting or sculpture; and so far as painting was concerned, the same was true of the Madras Museum and School of Art. The same attitude was traceable in the whole of the Government educational policy, in which Indian art and music were alike calmly and totally ignored. Take only one example, the teaching of drawing; no one had thought of studying indigenous methods, or making use of them. . . . The main difficulty seemed to be that English educationists in India wouldn't be brought to realize their own colossal ignorance. It seemed as if the English [mind was] not only indifferent to, and ignorant of, Indian art and music, but determined that Indians themselves should remain in equal ignorance.[11]

On the qualifications of European writers on Indian art, Coomaraswamy had equally strong views. These critics were usually archaeologists "or amateurs out of sympathy with the fundamental ideals of Indian thought". They were "prejudiced in some cases against Indian religion, and possessed of few of the faculties of appreciation and interpretation which are demanded of a writer on European art, they have found it most easy to condemn and criticize and have felt little or no consciousness of their duty to interpret".[12] For Coomaraswamy the writer of books on art ought to have essentially a different perception:

> The writer of books on art should aim to make his readers understand the art, to see the world as the artist saw it; at least, to know what the artist wished to say. Most writers on Indian art, in pointing out defects and limitations, have merely pointed out the obvious, and demonstrated the divergence of their own from the Indian point of view;

[11] Basu. op. cit., p. 129.

[12] Ibid.

> and the results could not be regarded as permanent contributions to the history of art. The European critic never seemed to penetrate behind the surface of an Indian sculpture and painting, or to have learnt its language; he did not perceive its intention, and, therefore, could not judge it. . . .[13]

These foreign writers did not know and could never really "feel the passion that animates many an Indian work of art; how then could they interpret or criticize?", Coomaraswamy asked his British audience. It was not that their "works had no value as records of historical fact" but it merely showed "that those who write, and those who accept such ideas, were not competent – as the Moguls or the Hindu rulers of India once were – to guide the art administration of the government".[14] The caution was direct, he spoke as a cultural-nationalist when he said:

> The British Government would be harshly judged by future generations for its philistine and ignorant indifference to Indian art and artists, and its policy would be unfavourably contrasted with that of the Hindu and Mogul rulers of the earlier, and in many respects, more cultured times.[15]

This neglect of the study of Indian culture and arts Coomaraswamy was, for "the essential error in modern Indian education". Such a neglect of the study of culture on the one hand and a convoluted understanding of it through the prevailing education system and methods on the other completely alienated the average Indian graduates from their own traditions:

> The most crushing indictment of this Education is the fact that it destroys, in the great majority of those upon whom it is inflicted, all capacity for the appreciation of Indian culture

13 Basu. op. cit., p. 129.

14 Ibid.

15 Ibid., p. 130.

> . . . the ordinary graduate of an Indian University is indeed a stranger in his own land.[16]

He was even more unsparing of the educated and Anglicized elite of his time.

> We, who think that we are educated and progressive, we, who attend conferences and sit on legislative councils, who are rulers of states, or earn princely incomes in courts of law, we ourselves have despised and hated everything Indian, and it is by that hatred that we have destroyed our industries and degraded the status of our artisans. . . . We never thought that the fault was in ourselves.[17]

Is the Indian graduate less of a stranger in his own land today; a century after Coomaraswamy had bemoaned his confused status, has the other section he referred to, realized where the fault lies?

In a discussion on *Music and Education in India* Coomaraswamy again referred to this omission of culture in education:

> the essential error in modern Indian education, as understood by Government, missionaries and Anglicized Indians is a refusal or inability to recognize any responsibility to the past. The consequent break in the continuity of the historical tradition is fatal to Indian culture.[18]

Indian arts and music was completely denied space in the official system of education, which "ignored" its importance.[19] Realising this lacunae Coomaraswamy advocated an education that would make use of the "national culture and national

---

16 *Essays in National Idealism*, pp. 96-97.

17 *Art and Swadeshi*, p. 11.

18 *Essays in National Idealism*, p. 186.

19 Ibid., pp. 187-88.

languages – literary, musical artistic – as the medium of instruction".[20]

A wider intellectual growth and awakening could come about "only by means of education in national culture".

But while talking for Indian culture and while creating himself into an ardent cultural nationalist, Coomaraswamy never lost sight of the world; his essential position saw no real contradiction between nationalism and internationalism – especially in terms of culture and the cultural right to be oneself. In the conflict "between the ideals of Imperialism and the ideals of Nationalism", Coomaraswamy the perennialist saw the need for India and Indian culture to survive so that they could contribute again to the cultures of the world:

> We believe in India for the Indians; but if we do so it is not merely because we want our own India for ourselves, but because we believe that every nation has its own part to play in the long tale of human progress, and that nations, which are not free to develop their own individuality and own character, are also unable to make the contribution to the sum of human culture which the world has a right to expect of them.[21]

And in the end, if India was to meaningfully contribute to the cultures of the world, to the civilizational advancement of humanity, she could best do it by remaining true to her essential identity – her cultural and spiritual identity – as Coomaraswamy stated in his seminal *The Dance of Shiva*:

> Each race contributes something essential to the world's civilization in the course of its own self-expression and self-realization. The character built up in solving its own problems, in the experience of its own misfortunes, is itself

---

[20] *Essays in National Idealism*, p. 193.

[21] Ibid., p. 2.

> a gift which each offers to the world. The essential contribution of India, then, is simply her Indianness. . . .[22]

Cautioning against the dangers of a "premature and artificial cosmopolitanism" and referring to other movements of the age when he was writing his cultural essays, Coomaraswamy called for a guard against such a diluting tendency:

> We do not stand alone in the awakening of our national genius; the phenomenon is worldwide, and may be studied in lands so far apart as Ireland and Japan. The movement is a protest of the human spirit against a premature and artificial cosmopolitanism which would destroy in nations . . . the special genius of each.[23]

Indian culture – a study of her arts and expressions – could help stem that and assist in expressing this Indianness – this special genius – and make it a palpable reality. Coomaraswamy's message as a cultural nationalist was indeed a wide one; in essence he saw India's culture as a grand avenue leading towards her integral awakening, he articulated the cultural dimension within the political debate of the age and inseparably linked the dimensions of political and cultural nationalism.

---

22 Ananda Coomaraswamy, "What Has India Contributed to Human Welfare" in *The Dance of Shiva*, p. 21.

23 *Essays in National Idealism*, p. vii.

3

Sri Aurobindo

Indian Culture and External Influence

ACTIVE in nationalist politics in the first decade of the last century, Sri Aurobindo (1872–1950), then Aurobindo Ghose, vigorously participated in the cultural debate of the epoch. In a series on "The National Value of Art" (1909) Sri Aurobindo dwelt at length on the need to impart artistic education and called for realizing its need in the new scheme of a national education in India. He also pointed at the gradual tendency in modern times to "depreciate the value of the beautiful and overstress the value of the useful".[1] Such a tendency, Sri Aurobindo argued, was "curbed in Europe by the imperious insistence of an agelong tradition of culture and generous training of the aesthetic perceptions"; but in India, where the people "had been cut off by a mercenary and soulless education from all [their] ancient roots of culture and tradition, it is corrected only by the stress of imagination, emotion and spiritual delicacy, submerged but not yet destroyed, in the temperament of the people".[2] And since these were submerged and not yet destroyed they could still be salvaged through a wide and effective training in aesthetics and culture. But the tendencies in the present age seemed to prevent the recognition of such a need, because, as Sri Aurobindo saw it,

---

1 Sri Aurobindo, "The National Value of Art", in *Complete Works of Sri Aurobindo* (*CWSA*), vol. 1, p. 433.

2 Ibid.

> the value attached by the ancients to music, art and poetry has become almost unintelligible to an age bent on depriving life of its meaning by turning earth into a sort of glorified antheap or beehive. . . .[3]

As one who was actively associated with the demand for the national control of education in India, between 1906 and 1910, Sri Aurobindo emphasized this aspect and, as his wont, saw it from the metaphysical and spiritual dimension of human growth. Stressing the need for aesthetic education in order to develop the spirit, he wrote:

> . . . a cultivated eye without a cultivated spirit makes by no means the highest type of man. It is precisely the cultivation of the spirit that is the object of what is well called a liberal education, and the pursuits best calculated to cultivate the growth of the spirit are language, literature, the Arts, music, painting, sculpture or the study of these, philosophy, religion, history, the study and understanding of man through his works and of Nature and man through the interpretative as well as through the analytic faculties.[4]

It was such a training in the arts that brought about a gradual process of "*chittashuddhi*", the "purification of heart", and in his focus on elevating man's nature, Sri Aurobindo indicated the precise role of such training:

> *Chittashuddhi*, the purification of the heart, is the appointed road by which man arrives at his higher fulfilment, and, if it can be shown that poetry and art are powerful agents towards that end, their supreme importance is established. They are that, and more than that. It is only one of the great uses of these things which men nowadays are inclined to regard as mere ornaments of life and therefore of secondary importance.[5]

---

3 Sri Aurobindo, "The National Value of Art", in *Complete Works of Sri Aurobindo* (*CWSA*), vol. 1, p. 433.

4 Ibid., p. 438.

5 Ibid., p. 445.

While arguing for developing an aesthetic education, Sri Aurobindo's essential question was "whether the sense of the beautiful has any effect on the life of a nation" and he obviously argued that it did and that the absence of qualities developed by such an education invariably became a source "of national weakness".[6] Drawing attention to the importance of painting and sculpture, like that of music, Sri Aurobindo saw the great necessity of developing an understanding of the need for a "universal proficiency in the arts and crafts" and in their appreciation:

> Plato in his *Republic* has dwelt with extraordinary emphasis on the importance of music in education; as is the music to which a people is accustomed, so, he says in effect, is the character of that people. The importance of painting and sculpture is hardly less. The mind is profoundly influenced by what it sees and, if the eye is trained from the days of childhood to the contemplation and understanding of beauty, harmony and just arrangement in line and colour, the tastes, habits and character will be insensibly trained to follow a similar law of beauty, harmony and just arrangement in the life of the adult man. This was the great importance of the universal proficiency in the arts and crafts or the appreciation of them which was prevalent in ancient Greece, in certain European ages, in Japan and in the better days of our own history. Art galleries cannot be brought into every home, but, if all the appointments of our life and furniture of our homes are things of taste and beauty, it is inevitable that the habits, thoughts and feelings of the people should be raised, ennobled, harmonised, made more sweet and dignified.[7]

---

6 Sri Aurobindo, "The National Value of Art", in *Complete Works of Sri Aurobindo* (*CWSA*), vol. 1, p. 446.

7 Ibid., p. 447. Coomaraswamy too made much the same point, when he wrote, "We have gone so far as to divorce work from culture, and to think of culture as something to be acquired in hours of leisure; →

Sri Aurobindo's call for seriously imparting "aesthetic education" was in line with Coomaraswamy's perception as well, both argued for the need to develop an awareness of and an education in culture. Both threw their weight behind the then crystallizing Bengal School of Art led by Abanindranath Tagore (1871–1951) and supported by E.B. Havell (1861–1934).

Throwing in his ideas and reading in this vigorous cultural debate, Sri Aurobindo dwelt at some length on "Indian Culture and External Influence", a much argued topic of the period. Sometime in March 1919, Sri Aurobindo, then nearly a decade into exile in the French enclave of Pondicherry, also joined the discussion. In the midst of writing his essays on the renaissance in India he wrote a paper in "answer to a comment in the Bengali journal *Narayana*" on his series.[8] In his point by point reply Sri Aurobindo argued that one had to be open – it was the demand of an age which saw an enhanced interaction between civilizations and continents – to wider influences and cultural waves of the world. Through an assimilation of those that were found to be assimilable India had to evolve newer creations based on her – to echo Coomaraswamy – *Indianness*. "Confronted with the huge rush of modern life and thought, invaded by another dominant civilization almost her opposite or inspired at least with a very different spirit to her own," Sri Aurobindo saw India surviving only "by confronting this raw, new, aggressive, powerful world with fresh diviner creations of her own spirit, cast in the mould of her own spiritual ideals."[9]

→ but there can be only a hothouse and unreal culture where work itself is not its means; if culture does not show itself in all we make we are not cultured." (*Oriental and Christian Philosophy of Art*, 1956, p. 15.)

[8] *CWSA*, vol. 20, 1997, p. 447. What that observation was remains un-elaborated in the notes on text of the volume.

[9] Ibid., p. 43.

She would have to solve the problems arising out of this situation "in her own way, through solutions arising out of her own being and from her own deepest and largest knowledge"[10] and this knowledge would have to come from or be inspired by the fundamentals of her traditions, of her culture. She could not shut herself out, but in order to steer her way through this rapidly evolving maze of modernity, she would have to be open to external cultural influences and yet handle them by delving deep within herself, within her *parampara*:

> I spoke of the acceptance and assimilation from the West of whatever in its knowledge, ideas, powers was assimilable, compatible with her [India's] spirit, reconcilable with her ideals, valuable for a new statement of life. This question of external influence and new creation from within is of very considerable importance. . . .[11]

The post-First World War world saw much discussion on the theme of a growing human unity. Sri Aurobindo examined much of this debate in his socio-political writings. Acknowledging the need to work towards trying to establish such an oneness, Sri Aurobindo, however, argued that such a unity, if it ever materialized, would be a dead one if it insisted on a uniform unity. In this vast exchange and interaction of culture, in this world, progressively growing close, it would perhaps be necessary to make sure that the push towards oneness ensured that the "principle of variation" was kept intact, that the fundamentals of one's civilizational and cultural identities survived. It was not by abolishing "ourselves, our own special temperament and power, that we can get at the living oneness, but by following it out and raising it to its highest possibilities of freedom and action".[12] Uniformity had

---

10 *CWSA*, vol. 20, 1997, p. 43.

11 Ibid.

12 Ibid., p. 44.

to be avoided, it killed life, "I have insisted", wrote Sri Aurobindo, "that uniformity is not a real but a dead unity: uniformity kills life while real unity, if well founded, becomes vigorous and fruitful by a rich energy of variation."[13] For him the debate on culture had to recognize the need for India to preserve her own cultural fundamentals while taking generously from the cultures of the world. Our early cultural nationalists, witness to cultural asymmetries during their days when the Empire and its cultural paradigms dominated, were themselves strong opponents of any mono-cultural trend.

Referring to the argument that a blind imitation does set in motion a process of degeneration and subjection for the imitating culture, Sri Aurobindo acknowledged a tendency to "make ourselves a sort of brown Englishmen" and found it a mistaken endeavour:

> That the attempt in the last century which still in some directions continues – to imitate European civilisation and to make ourselves a sort of brown Englishmen, to throw our ancient culture into the dust-bin and put on the livery or uniform of the West was a mistaken and illegitimate endeavour, I heartily agree.[14]

---

13 *CWSA*, vol. 20, 1997, p. 44.

14 Ibid., p. 45. In a seminal lecture "Swaraj in Ideas", philosopher and Sri Aurobindo's contemporary K.C. Bhattacharya (1875–1949) discussed the issue of cultural subjection as well. Bhattacharya's question was whether the assimilation happened "after a full and open-eyed struggle had been allowed to develop between it [external, foreign culture] and their [Indians] indigenous culture". Bhattacharya similarly described the general trend among the educated Indian towards the rediscovery of his cultural foundations, "It is admitted today – what was not sufficiently recognized in the earlier days of our Western education – that we had an indigenous culture of a high degree of development, the comparative value of which cannot be said to have been yet sufficiently appraised. Under the present system we generally receive Western culture in the first instance and then →

Sri Aurobindo, however, did not rant against such an imitation, and seeing the impossibility of an isolationistic existence and anticipating the revolutionary alterations in civilizational and cultural interactions, he realized that some amount of imitation would in any case occur. Especially, for a somnolent culture and people, the shock of contact with an active civilization and culture was needed. That process was to be repeatedly found in history. The position is best articulated in his own words:

> A certain amount of imitation, a great amount even, was, one might almost say, a biological necessity, at any rate a psychological necessity of the situation. Not only when a lesser meets a greater culture, but when a culture which has fallen into a state of comparative inactivity, sleep, contraction, is faced with, still more when it receives the direct shock of a waking, active, tremendously creative civilization, finds thrown upon it novel and successful powers and functionings, sees an immense succession and development of new ideas and formations, it is impelled by the very instinct of life to take over these ideas and forms, to annex, to enrich itself, even to imitate and reproduce, and in one way or in another take large account and advantage of these new forces and opportunities. That is a phenomenon which has happened repeatedly in history, in a greater or a lesser degree, in part or in totality.[15]

This section of his essays on the Indian renaissance remains a fascinating treatise in the comparative study of cultures.

→ we sometimes try to peer into our ancient culture as a curiosity and with the attitude of foreign oriental scholars and yet we say that this ancient culture of ours is no curiosity. Many of our educated men do not know and do not care to know much of this indigenous culture of ours, and when they seek to know, they do not feel, as they ought to feel, that they are discovering their own self." (K.C. Bhattacharya, "Swaraj in Ideas" in S.K. Ghosh ed., *Four Indian Critical Essays*, 1977, pp. 13-14.)

[15] *CWSA*, vol. 20, p. 45.

Interestingly, even here while discussing this phenomenon of imitation, Sri Aurobindo added an additional dimension. He differentiated between an imitation that is made after examination and deliberation and an imitation that is mechanical, made without much thought imparted to the cultural conditions and climate of the imitating people and land. He saw such a mechanical imitation initiating and accelerating this process of cultural degeneration. The way forward for subject cultures and civilizations was the recovery of their "own centre":

> If there is only a mechanical imitation, if there is a subordination and servitude, the inactive or weaker culture perishes, it is swallowed up by the invading leviathan. . . . To recover its own centre, find its own base and do whatever it has to do in its own strength and genius is certainly the one way of salvation.[16]

Without discounting the inevitability of some amount of imitation, Sri Aurobindo argued that a number of forms of expressions and of institutions in use did come to us from the West. What was however of a larger import was whether these could be modified by the characteristics of our own temperament and be given new directions and shape under its influence:

> A certain amount of acceptance, of forms too – some imitation, if all taking over of forms must be called imitation – is inevitable. We have, for instance, taken over in literature

[16] Ibid. Making a similar point Vivekananda once spoke to a group of young men on the need to avoid imitation "in toto": ". . . know it for certain, mere imitation will lead you nowhere. . . . You will be swept away from the moorings of your real life. . . . Imitation in toto is another form of slavery. What I mean is rational discrimination and assimilation of what is best in other countries and climes" (Bhupendranath Datta, *Swami Vivekananda: Patriot-Prophet*, 1954, pp. 333-34).

> the form of the novel, the short story, the critical essay among a number of other adoptions, in science not only the discoveries and inventions, but the method and instrumentation of inductive research, in politics the press, the platform, the forms and habits of agitation, the public association. I do not suppose that anyone seriously thinks of renouncing or exiling these modern additions to our life – though they are not all of them by any means unmixed blessings – on the ground that they are foreign importations. But the question is what we do with them and whether we can bring them to be instruments and by some characteristic modification moulds of our own spirit. If so, there has been an acceptance and an assimilation; if not there has been merely a helpless imitation.[17]

The entire effort ought to be, an attempt at an "assimilative appropriation – a making the thing settle into oneself and turn into characteristic form of our self-being".[18] In this, the necessity of never effacing one's uniqueness and originality was of paramount importance. In his inimitable style, Sri Aurobindo explained his stand on the entire process. Absent is any rancour or any exclusive call for a "return upon ourselves", the trends of a world, moving progressively closer, could not support such a claim. What was required, however, was to explore the possibilities of giving an "Indian treatment" to all that one came across during the course of this interaction:

> When I speak of acceptance and assimilation, I am thinking of certain influences, ideas, energies brought forward with a great living force by Europe, which can awaken and enrich our own cultural activities and cultural being if we succeed in dealing with them with a victorious power and originality, if we can bring them into our characteristic way of being and transform them by its shaping action. That was in fact

[17] *CWSA*, vol. 20, pp. 45-46.

[18] Ibid., p. 48.

> what our own ancestors did, never losing their originality, never effacing their uniqueness, because always vigorously creating from within, with whatever knowledge or artistic suggestion from outside they thought worthy of acceptance or capable of an Indian treatment.[19]

The process of "interchange" had come to stay and for Sri Aurobindo the "undesirability of total rejection" even if such a thing was possible, arose from the "fact that interchange with the environment is necessary to a healthy persistence and growth [and] the living organism which rejects all such interchange, would speedily languish and die of lethargy and inanition".[20] But it was also necessary to be self-possessed, to know oneself and one's own before being able to victoriously take on the wider world. As Sri Aurobindo put it:

> Those who live most powerfully in themselves, can also most largely use the world and all its material for the Self and, it must be added, most successfully help the world and enrich it out of their own being. The man who most finds and lives from the inner self, can most embrace the universal and become one with it; the *Swarat*, independent, self-possessed and self-ruler, can most be the *Samrat*, possessor and shaper of the world in which he lives, can most too grow one with all in the *Atman*.[21]

Such a stance was not in contradiction to the ideals of Indian culture, it never sought to isolate India from external influences, it rather marvelled at and examined whatever seemed new to her and attempted with a positive spirit to assimilate it to the spirit of her own cultural and social patterns:

> At no time did Indian culture exclude altogether external influences; on the contrary a very great power of selective

---

19 *CWSA*, vol. 20, p. 46.

20 Ibid., p. 48.

21 *CWSA*, vol. 20, p. 49.

> assimilation, subordination and transformation of external elements was a characteristic of its processes; it protected itself from any considerable or overwhelming invasion, but laid hands on and included whatever struck or impressed it and in the act of inclusion subjected it to a characteristic change which harmonized the new element with the spirit of its own culture.[22]

While writing in defence of Indian culture during this period, Sri Aurobindo produced a number of brilliant essays. At a time when Indian cultural nationalists perceived the cultural conflict intensifying, Sri Aurobindo's essays along with those of the Irish playwright and Indophile James Cousins (1873–1956), John Woodroffe and others provided the intellectual base to the entire cultural–nationalist discourse of the period. These protagonists and initiators of the renewed cultural debate in India examined the ongoing conflict of cultures and strongly felt that "India cannot afford to allow the case made against her to go unanswered".[23] She had to answer back the cultural assault in an awakened cultural idiom; it would not do to have an attitude of "superior disdain nor slothful negligence". As Woodroffe put it, "Attacks on Indian culture have led and will lead to its defence and appreciation.

But yet, while preparing for a cultural battle, our thinkers in question never allowed their vision to be clouded, they never lost sight of the fact that "mankind" was moving closer and thus, while arguing for Indian culture and for the need to revive in it an active Indian interest, they continued to talk of the need for Indian culture to not only renew its interactions with world cultures but to also explore how best it could adjust itself to newer world conditions and be responsive to the effects of a heightened global interaction.

---

22 *CWSA*, vol. 20, p. 50.

23 John Woodroffe, *Is India Civilised*?, pp. xxxv-xxxvi.

As Sri Aurobindo put it, while concluding his discussion of Indian culture and external influences:

> Nowadays any such strong separative aloofness as distinguished the ancient civilizations, is no longer possible; the races of mankind have come too close to each other, are being thrown together in a certain unavoidable life unity. We are confronted with the more difficult problem of living in the full stress of this greater interaction and imposing on its impacts the law of our being. . . . We cannot go backward to a past form of our being, but we can go forward to a large repossession of ourselves in which we shall make a better, more living, more real, more self-possessed use of the intervening experience. We can still think in the essential sense of the great spirit and ideals of our past, but the form of our thinking, our speaking, our development of them has changed by the very fact of new thought and experience; we see them not only in the old, but in new lights, we support them by the added strength of new viewpoints, even the old words we use acquire for us a modified, more extended and richer significance. . . .[24]

Writing at a time when the Western civilizational paradigm dominated Sri Aurobindo spoke of the need of an Asian assertion and formulated the essential issue when he wrote in conclusion:

> Finally, we cannot avoid dealing with the great governing ideas and problems of the modern world. The modern world is still mainly European, a world dominated by the European mind and Western civilization. We claim to set right this undue preponderance, to reassert the Asiatic and, for ourselves, the Indian mind and to preserve and develop the great values of Asiatic and of Indian civilization. But the Asiatic or the Indian mind can only assert itself successfully by meeting these problems and by giving them a solution

[24] *CWSA*, vol. 20, pp. 50-51.

which will justify its own ideals and spirit.[25]

The principle that he asserted, and which he felt to be a necessity for a much more complex global living in which culture would emerge as one of the main interactive dimensions, was to have:

> . . . fidelity to our own spirit, nature, ideals, the creation of our own characteristic forms in the new age and the new environment, but also a strong and masterful dealing with external influences which need not be and in the nature of the situation cannot be a total rejection.[26]

Sri Aurobindo saw the difficulty of really applying that principle – "the degree, the way, the guiding perception", but he presented a broad framework when he wrote, referring to the application of the principle:

> . . . we must look at each province of culture and, keeping always firm hold on a perception of what the Indian spirit is and the Indian ideal is, see how they can work upon the present situation and possibilities in each of these provinces and lead to a new victorious creation.[27]

Sri Aurobindo's interventions in the nationalist debate on culture introduced in it new and futuristic dimensions. He pushed for the thinking Indian mind to begin considering and debating the role that Indian culture and traditions would eventually play in the future national life and as an eloquent representative of the cultural nationalists he echoed their collective concern, and called for an essential cultural and spiritual repositioning.

---

25 *CWSA*, vol. 20, pp. 51-52.

26 Ibid., p. 52.

27 Ibid.

4

Sister Nivedita
Interpreting Indian Culture

ANOTHER dynamic figure of the period under discussion, who did much to revivify national interest in Indian art and culture, was the Hinduised Irish disciple of Swami Vivekananda, Sister Nivedita (Margaret Noble) (1867–1911). At the forefront of the early phase of the Indian nationalist movement Nivedita's action was multifaceted and she did much for the "national renaissance of Indian art". Through her school founded under the inspiration of Swami Vivekananda, through her writings on Indian themes and on Indian culture and through her formulations on Indian education, Nivedita contributed a great deal towards developing an awareness of Indian aesthetics. Like her contemporaries, Coomaraswamy and Sri Aurobindo, Nivedita wished to take the arts and culture to the people and reignite and preserve their artistic emotions. She once spoke vividly "of her dream of founding painting galleries" all over the country to further the mission of developing a greater cultural awareness and thirst:

> I have long thought that if I were an Indian prince I would use my surplus revenues first and foremost for the promotion of civic and historic painting. To this end I would open competitions and announce prizes, and establish picture-printing presses for cheap reproduction of coloured pictures. I would like to build open verandahs, running round three sides of a square, and bearing on their inner

> surfaces great mural pictures – some in pigments, some in mosaics, and some after the fashion of the Indian past, carved in stone in low relief – of the mighty scenes of the civic and national past. . . .[1]

These buildings which she preferred to call the "civic temples" or "temples . . . of the national spirit" would have inspiring scenes from the Indian past:

> . . . Ashoka sending forth his missionaries; Kanishka seated in council; Vikramaditya offering the Ashvamedha; the twelve crowned victims of Cheetore – the Coronation of Akbar; the building of the Taj – these, and such as these, should be the subjects here displayed, and every woman on her way to the river-*ghat*, and every labourer going to and from his work, should be made familiar with the idea of India, and the evolution of India through 4,000 years.[2]

Nivedita was convinced that a combination of the past historical–cultural memory could serve to reinforce not only a national sense in the people but would equally awaken their cultural sensitivity and quest. For Nivedita and her colleagues in the cultural nationalist movement the dissemination of the symbols of Indian culture was essential for developing and recreating a binding national unity with the focused goal of achieving freedom.

As emerges from their reading, our thinkers were not blind revisionists and did generously concede the need to develop an appreciation and understanding of other cultures as well, like Sri Aurobindo later, Nivedita too discussed at some length the "Place of Foreign Culture in a True Education". The cultural nationalism that these stalwarts championed did not propound a jealous isolationism or a culturally exclusivist mindset. In a short piece titled "From the National to the International"

---

1 *The Complete Works of Sister Nivedita* (CWSN), vol. 3, p. 58.

2 Ibid.

Nivedita discussed this issue which was then being vigorously debated. She clarified the stand of the cultural nationalists.

> People think that because we advocate Indian manners, or Indian art, or Indian literature, therefore we condemn European; because we preach an Eastern ideal, we despise a Western. Not so.[3]

The first need was a thorough-knowledge and discovery of what was "ours" before a thorough exploration and understanding could be undertaken of the other:

> . . . It would be a sin to bring up an Indian child on anything but the *Mahabharata*. But if he could not, when educated, appreciate the poetry of Homer, that fact would mean a limitation of his culture. A thorough training in our own ideals is the only preparation for an enjoyment of all. We learn our own, in order to enjoy all. . . . But we must not seek to reverse the process. We must not seek through Tennyson to produce the love of the *Ramayana*. Such shilly-shallying can induce only an imitative and bastard culture. Not by such training of poetic faculty can immortal literature ever again be written by us. Not even can there be perfect appreciation either of our own or foreign greatness.[4]

Nivedita's advocacy of the need to study and appreciate one's own culture before venturing out to study the other had been preceded by a phase when Indian scholarship of Indian culture was not taken seriously by Western Indologists. The phase was by no means over, and like others, Nivedita sought to challenge that assumption. This was a challenging phase for the "native" who aspired to become a scholar of his culture through an assiduous study of its various dimensions and facets. It was a period when Indian scholarship was assumed by the colonial Indologists to be innately inferior "in the field

---

[3] *CWSN*, vol. 5, p. 68.

[4] Ibid., pp. 69-70.

of Indian studies". The issue came to the fore in 1880s, especially with the advent of the Ilbert Bill introduced in 1883 which empowered Indian judges to try cases involving Europeans. The introduction of the Bill faced a barrage of opposition and the political angle was also projected through the cultural.

In his masterly study *Colonial Indology: Sociopolitics of the Ancient Indian Past*, Dilip K. Chakrabarti, for instances, directs attention to the cultural aspect of the protest to the Ilbert Bill and how it was used by some leading colonial indologists to summarily dismiss contributions of Indians to the study of Indian culture. The famous case was that of James Fergusson (1808-86), Scottish writer on Eastern and Indian architecture who criticized the works of the Indian Indologist Rajendralal Mitra (1823/24-1891). Fergusson argued that Mitra's works were mediocre and that the entire class that Mitra represented, the "*babus*" were in any case not capable of sustained scholarship and historical and cultural research and that it would not be wise to entrust people like him with juridical powers. Fergusson put the issue in perspective in his monograph, *Archaeology in India, with Especial Reference to the Works of Babu Rajandralala Mitra* (1884), when he derisively wrote:

> If, after reading the following pages, any European feels that he would like to be subjected to his [the *babus'* and Mitra as a representative of that class] jurisdiction, in criminal cases, he must have a courage possessed by few; or if he thinks he could depend on his knowledge, or impartiality, to do him justice, as he could on one of his own countrymen, he must be strangely constituted in mind, body and estate.[5]

---

[5] Cited in Dilip K. Chakrabarti, *Colonial Indology: Socio-Politics of the Ancient Indian Past*, 1997, p. 113.

In fact, Mitra's and Fergusson's encounters went back a long time in the past, as documented by one of Nivedita's leading biographers Sankari Prasad Basu. Referring to this debate, Basu points out that Mitra continuously refuted the notion that Indians learnt the usage of stone and bricks for building from Greeks especially after Alexander's invasion. He articulated this position much before the discovery of the remains of the Indus civilization. Mitra first wrote an article sometime in 1870 attacking such a notion; Fergusson challenged Mitra in a paper in the *Indian Antiquarian* in 1871. Mitra reiterated his stand in his *Antiquities of Orissa* leading Fergusson to write his *History of Indian and Eastern Architecture* (Sankari Prasad Basu, *Nivedita Lokmata*, vol. 4, p. 156). In his *Indo-Aryans* written in two volumes sometime in 1881, Mitra summed up his entire contention in the first lines, "It is generally believed that the oldest architectural remains to be seen India are the pillars of Ashoka, and they are not of a greater age than the middle of the third century before Christ. Hence it is, that an opinion is gaining ground that the ancient Aryans were not proficient in the art of building substantial edifices with stones, or brick, and that the early Hindus were dwellers in thatched huts and mud houses, or structures equally primitive" (Rajendralal Mitra, *Indo-Aryans*, vol. 1, 1881, p. 1). Fergusson, displaying the colonial Indologist's paternalizing attitude – especially of the Victorian type – argued in the introduction to his opus *History of Indian Architecture*, that India had never attained the intellectual and moral level of Greece and Rome, "It cannot, of course, be for one moment contended that India ever reached the intellectual supremacy of Greece, or the moral greatness of Rome". (James Fergusson, *History of Indian and Eastern Architecture*, vol. 1, 1910, p. 4.) Fergusson was not the only one to drum up theories of the architectural incapacities of Indians. There were other distinguished Indians who were equally swayed by this proposition. They failed to see any lofty inspiring conception or thought behind Indian architectural expressions. As for example did the legendary R.C. Dutt (1848–1909), who spent a lifetime studying and writing on Indian history and civilization. Dutt pretty much came to expound the same line when he referred to the lack of "lofty intellectual conception" in Indian architectural creation. In his *A History of Civilisation in Ancient India,* Dutt argued: "The wonderful edifices with which they [the Indian artisanal class] have covered India, under the bidding of the priest or the king, are remarkable, more for the gigantic labour and the minute and endless elaboration which they display, than for any lofty intellectual conception, any design of a creative mind. And among the thousands of graceful, pleasing, and natural figures and faces of men and women, which simple observation of nature taught the artisans to copy in stone in every temple and porch, we shall in vain seek for that high order of intellectual conception which marks the marbles of Greece and Rome. A Phoedias and a Michael Angelo were impossible in India." (R.C. Dutt, *A History of Civilisation in Ancient India,* vol. 2, 1893, p. 238.) Though Dutt wrote these lines long after the Fergusson–Mitra debate it nevertheless showed the tendency among a certain section of the Indian elite. In his essays defending Indian culture, Sri Aurobindo had quite bluntly asked, "Why are a certain class of Indians still hypnotized in all fields by European culture. . . ." He answered the question himself, it was because these Indians "constantly saw all the power, creation, activity on the side of Europe, all the immobility or weakness of a static, inefficient defence on the side of India" (Sri Aurobindo, "Is India Civilised"?, *CWSA*, vol. 20, p. 62).

Our interest is in the aspect of how Indian research and interest in Indian culture faced a tough challenge from the establishment of colonial Indologists. Fergusson selected two of Mitra's major contributions *The Antiquities of Orissa* in two volumes (1875, 1880) and *Buddha Gaya: the Great Buddhist Temple, the Hermitage of Sakya Muni* (1878) and spelt out why he had done so:

> Though Indian Archaeology may be considered as beneath the attention of the English public, the Ilbert Bill is certainly not so, and no means of bringing it home, and rendering it intelligible to the masses, appears to me so appropriate as examining a typical specimen of one of the proposed class of governors, and seeing what stuff they are made of. For this purpose there is probably no example so suitable as Babu Rajendralala.[6]

A fair appraisal of Mitra's research was not Fergusson's objective; he did his best to portray Mitra as one who hardly knew what he was writing and went to the extent of mocking his "Babu English".[7] Especially galling for Fergusson was Mitra's stand of refusing to "believe that India owed the origin of her stone architecture and sculpture to the Greeks". Referring to Mitra's stand, Fergusson was at his acerbic best when he wrote:

> His [Mitra's] patriotic soul was fired with uncontrolled indignation at the bare idea of his countrymen having taken a hint from foreigners, or borrowed a single idea from such a people as the Greeks.[8]

Mitra, on the other hand, in his inimitable style was equally tenacious in defending his stand and findings. In his *Indo-Aryans*, he referred to Fergusson's habit of blowing his top:

> Mr. Fergusson's remarks have not been of a comprehensive character, dealing with the subject in all its bearings, such as the public had a right to expect from a ripe scholar and

---

6 *Colonial Indology*, p. 113.

7 Ibid.

8 Ibid., p. 114.

> antiquarian of his standing. He seems to overlook, if not to ignore and repudiate, historical evidence, and to confine himself exclusively to the interpretation of ancient lithic remains . . . criticisms and abuse pure and simple have been, in regard to me, common enough in his writings for the last ten years, since I had the misfortune to dissent from his opinion regarding the Greek origin of Indian Architecture, and I do not wonder at them. They are, however, by no means ancillary to the ascertainment of truth, nor in any way remarkable as specimens of smart, sensational criticisms. . . . All ideas of literary amenity apart, sneers and revilings have never proved effectual substitutes for argument. They do not even suffice to suppress adverse opinion.[9]

In retrospect, observes Chakrabarti, both of Mitra's publications,

> . . . represent pioneering attempts in a number of directions: the study of the material basis of society on the basis of its representation in sculpture, the importance of the old canons of architecture in understanding its ancient specimens, and the role of the contemporary literary and inscriptional sources in understanding their historical contexts.[10]

Such a patronizing attitude *vis-à-vis* Indian scholarship was evident even later when Indian cultural nationalists began voicing an Indian response to study of Indian culture. At the "Conference for Orientalists" held at Simla in 1911, J.Ph. Vogel, then the officiating director general of the Archaeological Survey of India, for example, clearly expressed his doubts on the Indians' capacity of conducting archaeological research and study. In a note prepared "on the recruitment of officers for the Archaeological Survey" Vogel referred to works of

---

[9] Rajendralal Mitra, *Indo-Aryans*, vol. 1, pp. ii-iv.

[10] *Colonial Indology*, p. 113.

R.L. Mitra and others as not ranking in "equal with most" Western scholars.[11] Vogel saw the "prospects of Indian scholars taking a larger share in archaeological research" as not "very encouraging" because, as he argued, the Indians were apathetic towards their culture and history, the factors he traced were:

> The absence of historical sense among Indians, the undeveloped state of their artistic and aesthetic sense and the consequent inability on their part to appreciate beautiful specimens of sculpture, painting and architecture.

Chakrabarti adds that what Vogel left unsaid was that "he did not like the idea of Government of India archaeological jobs going out in any way of the control of European officers".[12]

Nivedita on her part robustly participated in this debate on the external influence on Indian art. She stoutly refused to accede to the notion that much of Indian art and architecture had actually developed under the influence of the Greeks. Whenever an opportunity presented itself Nivedita tried to refute these theories. She saw such a refutation as essential to the creation of an Indian discourse on the study of India. In her description of the "Ancient Abbey at Ajanta", for instance, she rejected the idea of a solely externally directed development of Indian art.

> Ordinarily speaking, we are accustomed to take for granted that an artistic style has arisen more or less in the neighbourhood of the place in which we find it. It requires no argument to convince us that Velasquez was the product of Spain or Titian or Venice. Even if we had not been informed of this we should have assumed it. To this rule, however,

---

[11] *Colonial Indology*, p. 115.

[12] Ibid.

> India has so far been an exception. The synthetic study of her past suffers from having been largely initiated by foreigners.[13]

For Nivedita it was the man "who knows least of Indian art at first hand, and is presumably most influenced by popular opinion, who delivers it over most cheerfully to a foreign origin and the assumption of native inadequacy and incompetence".[14] While framing her refutation of the theory, Nivedita described the two perceptions that then dominated the study of Indian art. The problem had to be clarified to the lay reader and Nivedita admirably described the contention: one theory argued that "from the beginning India had owed almost everything artistic to external forces". Under this schema the "Ashokan pillars were Persepolitan, the winged animals were Assyrian, the very lotuses and plant-forms were West Asian". And this school which "almost holds that India has no originality in matters of art, leans its own weight for the sources of her Buddhistic inspiration on the existence in Bactria, ever since the time of Alexander, of Greek artisan colonies".[15] It was from the descendants of Greek settlers, it argued, that "sprang the art of India." The other theory, especially bearing on the "evolution of the statue of Buddha as a sacred image" also suffered from a slanted take. These sacred images of the Buddha, it argued,

> was not an Indian invention. The idea was first conceived in the country of Gandhara, the contact-point between India and the West.[16]

For Nivedita, an articulate and aggressive advocate of Indian culture, India was already a global force long before her contact with Western civilization. In a remarkable allusion to this

13 *CWSN*, vol. 4, p. 66.

14 Ibid., p. 67.

15 *CWSN*, vol. 4, p. 68.

16 Ibid.

globalization of Indian culture and Indian thought, Nivedita argued that their world reach had long preceded Alexander's Eastern adventure. India had already begun to influence civilizations on her West, the exchange and commerce of culture was never a one-sided affair:

> . . . We cannot admit that Alexander created these routes [ancient trade routes]. That had been done silently through the ages that preceded him by the footsteps of merchants and pilgrims, of traders and scholars and even monks. The fame of Indian philosophy in the West had preceded Alexander. Indian thinkers had long gone, however few and far between, in the wake of Indian merchants . . . it is possibly true that before the raid there had been very little compensating back-flow into India.[17]

Therefore the Buddha images were very much the products of an Indian mind and imagination. Leading the discussion into a wide narrative of civilizational intercourse, Nivedita continued to argue against the theory of an overwhelming external influence on Indian architecture whenever the occasion presented itself.[18]

Against a prevailing atmosphere of resistance to Indians' studying India, Nivedita closely associated herself in creating a group of young Indian nationalist scholars who assiduously began to equip themselves for the study of India. Apart from a huge output of popular work on Indian art and culture, Nivedita herself made great efforts towards supporting such a group in its effort to achieve sturdy academic credentials. In a note to some of them on "What Books to Read" she made certain insightful observations on the "study of India" by urging them to develop a spirit that would go to the origin of any study or report on India. In the study of India, she argued

---

[17] *CWSN*, vol. 4, p. 69.

[18] See her detailed discussion in ibid., pp. 87-91.

there were "thousand directions" in which one could specialize:

> We may study India with a view to understanding races, or minerals, or agriculture or industry, or history, or literature or philosophy, or any one of an infinite number of subjects, but from one thing we have to emancipate ourselves and that is, from the idea that very much is yet known on the subject. We have to study the origin of the reports which reach us rather than those reports themselves. Those reports are, for the most part mere resumes turned out with political intention and mechanical lifelessness, and no true history was ever written in that way.[19]

This group of young nationalist scholars was to soon produce a prolific research output on the theme of Indian culture and history by trying to reinterpret the entire gamut of Indian civilization from the Indian nationalist point of view. Acharya Satish Chandra Mukherjee (1865–1948), founder of the Dawn Society and one of the leading educationists of the period who worked for the popularization of the study of Indian culture through his journal, *The Dawn Society's Magazine,* influenced this group by providing them a platform to conduct research and publish their papers.[20] One of the leading lights in this group,

---

[19] Sister Nivedita, *Selected Essays*, 1911, p. 202.

[20] Satish Chandra's magazine in fact regularly devoted an entire section named "Indiana" to the study of Indian history and culture. Satish Chandra himself published numerous papers on the theme in the magazine and "inspired his pupils to carry on intensive studies and investigations into historical subjects". According to one of his pupils, social scientist Benoy Kumar Sarkar (1887–1949) it was during this period that Satish Chandra encouraged young scholars to undertake research on India and South-East Asia. Radhakumud Mookerjee, a professor of history at the Bengal National College during this period (January 1909), produced his paper "The Wonderful Unity of India: A Deeper View" which led to the publication of his celebrated *The Fundamental Unity of India* in 1914. Another of Satish Chandra's pupils who took advantage of the Dawn forum, Haran Chandra Chakladar, →

the historian Radhakumud Mookerjee (1884–1964) articulated the nationalist academic spirit of the age, when he wrote:

> . . . It is high time that a school of scholars should grow up who will devote themselves assiduously to the sacred task of vindicating the ancient culture of the country, which was not at all found wanting in the matter of promoting the harmonious development of the entire nation in all the manifold fields of human activity, material and moral, secular and spiritual, physical and religious.[21]

As one of the leading advocates of the Bengal School of Art, Nivedita greatly encouraged and supported the efforts of young painters such as Abanindranath Tagore (1871–1951) in trying to rediscover their indigenous artistic roots and inspiration. In this advocacy too, her approach was that of the cultural nationalists of the age, who did not shut themselves to new creative impulses and currents. For her, though India was not "to hark back to the old ways" in matters of art and "refuse to consider or adopt anything that is new" she would have to at the same time train her people, her aspiring artists in the Indian art-conventions "through Indian associations". In this it was "worse than useless to desire to speak to them through the conventions and associations of Italy or Greece".[22] Nivedita encouraged the members of her young artistic team

→ later author of the work *Social Life in Ancient India* also wrote a number of papers during the period under discussion. Some of his papers such as, "Maritime Activity and Enterprise in Ancient India: Intercourse and Trade by Sea with China" and "Ship-Building and Maritime Activity in Bengal", which appeared between 1910 and 1912 were widely appreciated in nationalist circles and among the international readership of the magazine as well. (Haridas and Uma Mukherjee, *The Origins of the National Education Movement*, 2nd edn., 2000, pp. 237-38.)

21 Radhakumud Mookerjee, *Nationalism in Hindu Culture*, 1921, p. 88.

22 *CWSN*, vol. 3, p. 6.

to rediscover the Indian painting; she was clear on the essence of such a painting and also of the training and temperament that would inspire such an indigenous work:

> An Indian painting, if it is to be really Indian and really great, must appeal to the Indian heart in an Indian way, must convey some feeling or idea that is either familiar or immediately comprehensible; and must further, to be of the very highest mark, arouse in the spectator a certain sense of a revelation for which he is the nobler. [And to do this it was clear] that it must be made of elements which in themselves are already approved by the communal taste. Thus an Indian man who has studied the carved stone doorways of Orissa, or the beaten silver of Southern temples has already possessed himself of a great language of the beautiful, and when he speaks in that language, in India, he will be understood by all, and outside India by those who are sufficiently trained, or sufficiently gifted. Now this language he will speak to perfection, because he himself will understand every line and curve of it. But will he be as competent to represent, say a Gothic window, as he is to draw an Orissan exterior?[23]

It was essential that the Indian artists of the new age, inspired by the visions of a rising cultural nationalism find their inspiration and defining technique within their cultural and civilizational experience, the *swadeshi* art movement of which Nivedita was one of the principal shapers essentially made this point.

Under the inspiration of these cultural nationalists attempts were made by these inspired groups to undertake an assiduous and scientific study of Indian culture, heritage and traditions. The orientalized image of a solely mystic India had to be challenged, and Indian culture and its study served as a major instrument in articulating that challenge.

---

[23] *CWSN*, vol. 3, pp. 6-7.

Nivedita provided a fillip to the entire cultural debate of the period. Her contribution to the study of Indian art and culture, and to the popularization and Indianization of their study was recognized in a tribute to her by Abanindranath Tagore when he acknowledged her work in opening the "eyes of the Indians to the beautiful in their country, their own art and their own institutions".[24] Another of her associates, the art historian and critic O.C. Gangoly (1881–1974), referring to Nivedita's contributions, feelingly observed:

> It was a God-given faculty which enabled her to unlock the mystery of Indian culture. . . . She set down her own reactions to Indian culture and civilisation in her great book *The Web of Indian Life*. This book, full of brilliant expositions has provided Indians with new spectacles through which to look at our own culture in the new meanings and significances. . . . She was the first to admire the new masterpieces of Indian painting produced by Abanindranath Tagore and Nandalal Bose [(1882–1966)]. . . . She took Nandalal Bose to copy the world famous frescoes of the Ajanta Caves and helped the great artist to recover his great spiritual heritage. . . .[25]

Coomaraswamy came most near the truth in his assessment of Nivedita's contribution to the cultural debate, when he wrote in his preface to the *Myths of the Hindus and the Buddhists* that through her work and cultural advocacy, Nivedita

> became not merely an interpreter of India to Europe, but even more, the inspiration of a new race of Indian students, no longer anxious to be Anglicized, but convinced that all real progress, as distinct from mere political controversy, must be based on national ideals, upon intentions already clearly expressed in religion and art.[26]

24 *Lokmata*, vol. 4, p. 114.

25 Ibid., p. 241.

26 Ananda Coomaraswamy, *Myths of the Hindus and the Buddhists*, 1920, p. v.

5

John Woodroffe
Defending Indian Culture

ANOTHER curious Western figure who had adopted and internalized "eternal India" and joined the debate on culture was John Woodroffe (1865–1936). A prolific writer on Indian cultural issues and a leading interpreter of Indian Tantrism, Woodroffe welcomed all external challenges to Indian cuture. In his rather provocatively titled, *Is India Civilised*? (1918) he elucidated why:

> By continual assaults, often of a contemptuous and abusive character, this country is being gradually goaded into an active defence of its culture. And it is well that it should be so. . . . If India is aroused from its lethargy thereby, such attacks, however unjust they may be in themselves, will serve a useful purpose so far as this country's culture is concerned.[1]

Woodroffe advocated the need for an active defence in the face of an external assault on the understanding of Indian culture. He refuted the habit of misapplying the doctrine of "non-resistance" to this situation:

> He who is in and of the world will protect himself by action. It is necessary for all to defend with sincerity what is of worth in the inheritance got from their forefathers if they

[1] John Woodroffe, *Is India Civilised*?, 3rd edn., 1922, pp. 55-56.

> would escape the death which shadows degenerate descendants.[2]

Those who wished to "desert their cultural inheritance for some supposed political advantage"[3] would do so at the peril of completely derecognizing themselves.

Discussing the "Cultural Attack on India" Woodroffe discerned a "political motive" behind this habit of hostile criticism. The motive was to try and prove that "notwithstanding claims and appreciations to the contrary India [was] unqualified for the political advancement which, She seeks". Such a false view, Woodroffe argued, was seriously held by a section of the Western public because of their massive ignorance of India's culture:

> Ignorance of the true character of Indian civilization is such, and it has been so misrepresented, that the bulk of Western people may well believe that they are also serving both the interests of themselves and this country by cultural dominance.[4]

It was a reference to the sense of the "mission civilisatrice"[5] that Westerners held when it came to their colonies. But, it was

---

[2] *Is India Civilised?*, p. 57.

[3] Ibid., p. 64.

[4] *Is India Civilised?*, pp. 142-43. Referring to William Archer's book *India and the Future* (1917), in response to which he wrote his essays, Woodroffe summarized the entire attitude of the Western controller of culture *vis-à-vis* his Indian subject, in short, he defined "the political basis of the cultural attack": "Give up yourselves. Be like us. If you do, you have our support for 'your political aspirations'. You will not get it if you persist in your barbarism." (Woodroffe, *Is India Civilised?*, p. xliii.)

[5] Referring to this civilizing mission syndrome Coomaraswamy once caustically remarked, "What you call your "civilizing mission" is in our eyes nothing but a form of megalomania. Whatever we need to learn from you, we shall come to ask you for as the need is felt. At the →

not the Westerner alone who could be blamed for possessing such an attitude, educated Indians, Woodroffe argued, were to be equally blamed for being indifferent to their culture:

> If their [Westerners] belief be either wholly or partially wrong, the Indian people are largely to blame for this result, because the English-speaking section of them have been indifferent to the defence and exposition of their culture, where they have not actually neglected, depreciated, or condemned it.[6]

It was not sufficient to remain passive, what was required was an active defence, a voluble talking back on the issues of culture, especially because the attacks on Indian culture were often "either unscrupulous in spirit or inaccurate in fact". The objective of such criticism was quite simple and Woodroffe took the Western detractors of Indian culture head-on in laying bare their propelling motive. It provided a clear insight into the politics of culture then being fought out in colonial India. If India's face could be made "ugly" then the case for self-determination would surely suffer a debilitating blow:

> It is obvious that if it can be established that India . . . is not civilized but barbarous, that is an argument against Her capacity for political autonomy. If Her face can be made ugly, religiously, morally, intellectually and socially and in every other way, then the British people will not like the look of it. In the meanwhile do not let them be deluded by the idea that She has real civilized worth. She is barbarous. If other Western critics, judging the matter without political bias, have approved any form of Indian culture, steps must be taken to discredit them and to show they are all wrong or interested.[7]

→ same time, if you choose to visit us, you will be welcome guests, and if there is anything of ours that you admire, we shall say, "It is yours". . ." . (Ananda K. Coomaraswamy, *The Bugbear of Literacy*, 1947, p. 11.)

6. *Is India Civilised?*, p. 143.

7. Ibid., pp. 144-45.

Woodroffe actively participated in trying to alter this perception of India and her systems. He expressed an apprehension, however, of seeing the governing principles of Indian civilization, productive of the essentials of Indian character, suffer defeat in the country of their origin. Interestingly, he saw this happening not so much by "foreign hands *but at its own*",[8] he saw it coming for long:

> I have long foreseen and said . . . never has it been in such a danger as at the present time, when disruptive forces alien to the true Indian spirit have commenced their work. Those who have hitherto failed to perceive the necessity for the preservation of Indian tradition may yet live to see the ripened fruit of their misjudgment or negligence.[9]

For preserving these traditions, Woodroffe argued for the need to include the study of Indian culture in a systematic and comprehensive manner in the school curriculum. Supporting the demands of the national education movement, he called for admitting:

> . . . the claim of the true Indian patriot that his language, history, literature, art, philosophy, religion, general culture and ideals be given the primary place in the prescribed courses of study.[10]

The issue with Woodroffe was not "whether the English language and culture should be taught, but whether the Indian culture should be neglected".[11] It was known "how little value was attached to anything Indian by Macaulay, the protagonist of English culture" in the past, and Woodroffe saw many,

---

[8] John Woodroffe, *Bharata Shakti: Collection of Addresses on Indian Culture*, 3rd edn., 1921, p. xlvi.

[9] Ibid., pp. xlvi-xlvii.

[10] Ibid., pp. 79-80.

[11] John Woodroffe, *The Seed of Race: An Essay on Indian Education*, 1919, p. 33

"perhaps most" continuing to share and propagate "sometimes in tempered form", Macaulay's views.[12] An acute sense of inferiority had been allowed to colour the young Indians' way of looking at themselves, and through a strong and continuous suggestion of his inferiority his "spirit of self-assertion" was battered down:

> He has been told that he has had no glorious past, that the history of his country is lacking in great personalities, that the "progressive" West is superior to the "immobile" East and its old-world civilization and so forth, and that therefore his only chance of making himself the equal of Western peoples is by giving up his "Barbarism". . . and making himself as like his civilized Western teachers and rulers as possible. If day in and day out, suggestions of his innate inferiority are made to a boy, and the superiority of a foreign civilization is affirmed, he will, according to every probability, come to depreciate his own people and culture. This is what has happened. . . .[13]

An erasure of this sense of inferiority could come about, prosposed Woodroffe, through a rigorous cultural education. It disturbed him to see that there was nothing Indian in the entire orientation of schools that functioned under the official system, it would not do for young Indian minds to "forget their own" while learning all about others:

> I have recently read a prospectus of studies for an Indian school, in which there was not a single item which showed that the boys were Indian. By all means, let them learn about, and be helped by, the example of other countries, but let them not forget their own. If they took what others could give, let them assimilate it so that it became not others, but their own.[14]

---

12 *The Seed of Race*, p. 33

13 Ibid., pp. 33-34.

14 *Bharata Shakti*, p. 51.

But for this change of outlook to happen in the Indian education system, its responsibility, Woodroffe pointed out, had to be increasingly placed in the hands of the "*right type* of Indian" and by that he meant a "man who has knowledge of, and reverence for, his civilization and will carry it forward with devotion to truth".[15]

In line with the Indian culture nationalists, Woodroffe did not advocate a clash with the external penetrating culture; his was an advocacy which argued for being allowed to be first what one was. The notion of civilizational superiority had to be discarded:

> It is not necessary to enquire into the question of the respective superiority of the civilizations of East and West. It is sufficient to hold that Indian civilization is the best for the people whose forefathers have evolved it. Let us stop all attempts, direct or indirect whether political or religious, to impose our beliefs and practices on a people to whom they are foreign.[16]

Moreover in the present circumstances such a mentality of clash and isolation was in reality quite unfeasible, defending his position, Woodroffe argued against the perception which saw "any one who had a word to say in favour of Indian culture" as favouring "segregation" and "separatism".[17] He saw all separatism becoming increasingly difficult, in the present and the future world. Knowledge was becoming universal, and it would be ideal if more and more Indians came to know of the world without compromising their essential "organism":[18]

---

15 *The Seed of Race*, pp. 30-31.

16 *Bharata Shakti*, p. 79.

17 *The Seed of Race*, p. 32.

18 Ibid., pp. 32-33. Woodroffe clarified his stand and his contentions when he wrote, "... I urge reaction against *subjection* to foreign cultural influences. This does not mean that what is foreign and useful and →

As I have argued earlier, it is interesting to reflect upon the fact that our thinkers under discussion were rarely promoters of an exclusive cultural nationalism. While talking for their culture and the need for cultural recognition and autonomy, these thinkers deftly transcended the East–West binary. Their cultural nationalism was never predatory or aggressive in nature and essentially argued for the right to culturally be oneself in a culturally diverse global order.

While talking for the national they appear to have always kept the international in mind, never wanting to shut India off from the larger world and its developments. They encouraged and championed the interactions of ideas, cultures and civilizations, they saw such exchanges as enriching the Indian identity. But such a process of mutual enrichment could effectively take place only if it happened based on a firm foundation of one's own ways of being. Such a foundation was essential to avert confusion as Woodroffe characteristically put it in the end:

> In perfecting our forms we approach to others who have perfected theirs. The highly intellectual, moral, and spiritual are everywhere akin, and this, is as a friend of mine calls it, "the International of Culture". It is not to be obtained by neglect of one's own *Dharma* and by taking a bit here and a bit there to make up some combination which is neither "fish, flesh, fowl, nor even good red herring".[19]

In any case for Woodroffe the question of the value of Indian culture was not "merely an academic one". It had "present practical bearing on the future of India and the World". "Everyday," he wrote, "I ponder upon, and question myself

→ good may not be *assimilated*. Western civilization is a great, though a different, civilization from which much may be learnt. But to assimilate one must first be a strong free personality" (Woodroffe, *Is India Civilised*, p. liii).

19 *Bharata Shakti*, p. 129.

as to, the future of this country. Will it preserve its essential character, that is culture?"[20] Woodroffe left the debate open, he left it to the people of his adopted land "to say where they will go" but he did exude a certain confidence that India would eventually find the "Indian way":

> What I urge is that the Indian Spirit should *be itself* and thus have *cultural freedom*. When it has regained this, by the study and appreciation of its own inherited ancient and grand culture, and by the casting away of all unassimilated foreign borrowings, it may go where it will. I have confidence that in such case, its way will be a right way – that is an Indian way.[21]

Throughout their political struggle, Indian nationalists perceived the necessity of developing a cultural response with the hope that it would supplement their political and social struggle. They also hoped that this cultural response would gradually be yielded greater space and scope once the occupiers left and India was free to reshape her national life in full freedom. Woodroffe in his defence of Indian culture essentially radiated that hope.

---

20 *Is India Civilised?*, pp. xlv-xlvi.

21 Ibid., pp. lv-lvi.

Part II

6

K.M. Munshi
Reintegrating Indian Culture

SOME among our founding fathers were not mere theoreticians or sermonizers on the Indian need for cultural activism but had in fact, quite early, begun creating institutions and envisaging the route ahead for recreating a culturally conscious and vibrant India. The now marginalized nationalist statesman and cultural maven, K.M. Munshi (1887–1971), was an avant-garde in this respect. Munshi was the one to conceive and execute what can easily pass off as one of the grandest projects undertaken in independent India for the restoration and rejuvenation of Indian culture. It is interesting to note how leaders such as him found time, in the midst of their frenetic political activities, to tune in to the deeper spirituo-cultural dimensions of India and to labour towards giving these expressions under modern conditions. The story of the Somanatha Temple restoration is too well known and has been often reiterated in the past. What I wish to focus on and understand is Munshi's larger plan behind the project. It appears, that he wished to develop the entire area into a vibrant cultural and educational centre that would, in the long run, reflect and symbolize facets of India's culture and history during a particularly rich phase.

Munshi, who had been writing about Gujarat's historic past since 1910 had by 1922 already envisaged the need to re-create the mighty Somanatha Temple in Saurashtra and to preserve for posterity the sacred spot of *dehotsarga* where Sri Krishna was said to have "shuffled off his mortal coil". His widely read novel *Jaya Somanatha* which appeared in 1937 pushed the cause for recreating the temple by vividly painting the entire historic canvas of the age when the temple had stood as a mighty symbol of spiritual, cultural and material wealth of the Indian people.[1] In 1938 Munshi founded the Bharatiya Vidya Bhavan in Bombay in order to spearhead and popularize the study and research of Indian culture, history and civilization. The Vidya Bhavan remained for long a flagship institution giving direction to the cultural life of the country during the liberation struggle and later. Munshi was thus one of those leaders who, while in the thick of nationalist politics, still continued to remain culturally prolific and active displaying infinite patience and dexterity in juggling onerous public responsibilities with an effective cultural action.

Seeking to draw inspiration from others for his proposed project of reviving Somanatha, Munshi wrote to his erstwhile mentor and former professor at Baroda College, "Professor Arvind Ghosh", saying that he had been working for the reintegration of Indian culture and needed strength to carry forward the message of the "Seers". Sri Aurobindo replying in the affirmative assured his former student that he was right in "feeling that there should be reintegration of Indian culture under modern conditions". It was "*the*" work that had to be done.[2] Interestingly, the original plan of the Somanatha reconstruction seemed to symbolize just such an effort at reintegration.

---

1 K.M. Munshi, *Somanatha: The Shrine Eternal*, pp. 61-62.

2 Munshi had written to Sri Aurobindo on 30 July 1950 seeking guidance on the "future of Sanatan Dharma" and regarding his own work for Indian culture. Sri Aurobindo dictated the reply to A.B. Purani (1894–1965) a former political associate of Munshi then settled in Pondicherry and sent it under Purani's signature. (Sri Aurobindo, *Autobiographical Notes and Other Writings of Historical Interest*, 2006, p. 513.)

Nehru's misgivings and suspicion notwithstanding, the work of resurrecting the temple continued till the project saw final completion in 1965. The entire exercise of executing the project threw up a variety of issues and debates, and became a remarkable instance in the field of cultural conservation and renewal. The issue was not seen as merely one of reconstructing a temple under the influence of religious sentiment; Munshi's original plan had a much wider vision and included the development of the legendary pilgrim town of Prabhas which had by then "fallen into neglect", the raising of a monument at *dehotsarga,* the setting up of a seat of learning which would be developed into a university and the creation of a model agricultural and dairy farm on the lines of the Institute of Agriculture at Anand. The objective was to include

> not only the rebuilding and the maintenance of the Somanatha Temple itself and its auxiliary institutions . . . but also the general improvement of the neighbourhood so as to restore its atmosphere of sanctity.[3]

People could visit the area for worship, health, study as well as rest. Munshi envisioned the creation of a compact cultural hub that would, while seeking to re-create the glory of the ancient religious seat, develop itself into a pulsating centre for the study of Indian culture.

Regarding the need for developing a centre of learning as part of the project, Munshi argued that a "temple by itself would not be enough" and that usually the "authoritative tradition of a great temple" did not "permit its disassociation from a centre of learning" and therefore the creation of such a centre[4] would be entirely in consonance with the overall identity and past renown of the place as being sacred in the cultural history of India.

---

[3] *Somanatha: The Shrine Eternal*, p. 72.

[4] Ibid.

In a detailed note to his other inspirer in the project, Vallabhbhai Patel, Munshi proposed the setting up of a Central Sanskrit University in the vicinity that would encourage research in the ancient traditions of India – linguistic and cultural – and would by "preserving the best in the old methods" of teaching then followed by the indigenous Sanskrit learning centres (*pathashalas*) reorient the "out-of-date courses and keep alive the inspiration of Sanskrit and all it stands for in the life and learning of the country".[5] Through the project Munshi envisaged the creation of an entirely new cultural centre in India. To him Somanatha's history of being one of the "greatest seats of learning presided over by great teachers" made the idea of a centre of education extremely relevant.[6] He argued that since a growing number of international scholars were coming to India in order to study her culture, "a place where Sanskritic learning is co-ordinated with modern learning will attract attention all over the world".[7] Munshi also wished for this attached project to eventually have an all-India characteristic, and saw it as an all-India cultural asset and a world asset. He made it a point to specifically note that "a mere parochial institution confined to Western India" would be "of no value; to be a world asset, it must be an All India University".[8]

On the inspirational plane, Patel, appears to have been categorical on the intrinsic value of the entire project, he felt that the people "would never genuinely feel that freedom had come, nor develop faith in [their] future, unless Somanatha was restored".[9] Interestingly, decades earlier, Swami Vivekananda

---

5 *Somanatha: The Shrine Eternal*, pp. 73-74.

6 Ibid., p. 74.

7 Ibid., p. 75.

8 Ibid.

9 Ibid., p. 85.

had made a similar point regarding this cycle of temple reconstruction and its symbolism in relation to the Hindu psyche and had specifically referred to the Somanatha Temple in this context. In his speech on the "Future of India", the Swami while discussing religion as a cardinal strength providing pillar of Indian national life reminded his audience:

> Your forefathers underwent everything boldly, even death itself, but preserved their religion. Temple after temple was broken down by the foreign conqueror, but no sooner had the wave passed than the spire of the temple rose up again. Some of these old temples of southern India and those like Somnath of Gujarat will teach you volumes of wisdom, will give you a keener insight into the history of the race than any amount of books. Mark how these temples bear the marks of a 100 attacks and a 100 regenerations, continually destroyed and continually springing up out of the ruins, rejuvenated and strong as ever! That is the national mind, that is the national life-current.[10]

The symbolism of Somanatha had inspired some of the most influential Indian minds over the ages, unlike its physical structure, its memory and mysticism did not cease to generate hope of a civilizational recovery. Those at the forefront of the reconstruction project in modern times appeared to be simply continuing that ancient religio-cultural cycle. The effort did

---

[10] Swami Vivekananda's talk "Future of India" delivered at Madras, *CWSV*, vol. 3, p. 289. In his *Somanatha and Other Mediaeval Temples in Kathiawar*, Henry Cousens (1854–1933) some time superintendent of the Archaeological Survey of India, Western Circle, referred to this unique cycle of destruction and resurrection, "Many a time has its wall borne the brunt of battle and been levelled by the hand of the barbarian invader, only to rise again from its ashes, like the phoenix, as soon as the enemy had turned his back. The banner of Shiva was again raised aloft above its pinnacle; and the bells, the conch, and the drum once more announced the resumption of worship within." (*Somanatha and other Mediaeval Temples in Kathiawar*, 1931, p. 11.)

fig. 6: Somanatha Temple, with the "large Musalman dome". Photo by F. Nelson, *c*. 1895. Courtesy: British Library Online Gallery

not appear to them to be alien to the Indian mind or in contradiction to the functioning of her modern polity.

Munshi, in a letter to Nehru, movingly described the deeper *raison d'être* of the project and the innate reason for his involvement in it:

> . . . It is my faith in our past which has given me the strength to work in the present and to look forward to our future. I cannot value freedom if it deprives us of the *Bhagavad-Gita* or uproots our millions from the faith with which they look upon our temples and thereby destroys the texture of our lives. I have been given the privilege of seeing my incessant dream of Somanatha reconstruction come true. That makes me feel – makes me almost sure – that this shrine once restored to a place of importance in our life will give to our people a purer conception of religion and a more vivid

> consciousness of our strength, so vital in these days of freedom and its trials.[11]

It is difficult to find such earnest expressions in our present political-cultural climate and in the whittled down monochromatic discourse that it tends to impose. Munshi's noble sentiments apart, the entire project was by itself a rather unique model in the field of cultural and heritage conservation. It did offer an indigenous alternative in that field, in tune with the land's civilizational ethos and spiritual nature. The entire effort does not seem to have received sufficient recognition or acknowledgement, nor did it inspire other efforts that would replicate such projects in other regions. The compulsion to see the entire project as yet another majoritarian revivalist effort seems to have discouraged any inclination to study its varied dimensions in the true spirit of the learner for implementation or replication in the field of Indian cultural conservation and popularization.

Apart from his massive effort at rebuilding the temple, Munshi was himself a thinker and debater on culture and ceaselessly examined the present and the future of Indian culture. Like a number of his contemporaries who had participated in the liberation struggle Munshi too saw the need to have a firm grounding in the foundations of Indian culture. In a discussion he once described the crisis of the age as he saw it, he told his young audience:

> In these days, when you are going to be called upon to build a nation, if your feet are not planted on the foundations of our culture, you will be just "foreigners" as were the English members of the old Indian Civil Service. Without any roots in the soil, you will never be able to understand what our people are and what they want, nor would you be able to

---

11 Munshi's letter to Nehru dated 24 April 1951 in K.M. Munshi, *Pilgrimage to Freedom*, p. 564.

> judge what they would assimilate, and why. . . . I know how difficult it is for you to vitalize your roots in the soil. Today few of our educated young men are given a living faith in our great past through any influence at home. Our university education has also been depriving them of an insight into our culture. . . .[12]

Like many of his generation Munshi himself had undergone a phase of struggle and self-doubt when it came to understanding the essentiality of Indian culture in India's national life and before that in trying to understand what Indian culture itself signified. As he recalled:

> I was in the college and like some of you, we thought ourselves "progressives" only when we looked down on our ancient heritage, and looked up to whatever came from the West. . . . The question that slowly began to confront me and that insisted on being answered was: "How was it that Indian Culture had survived when so many ancient cultures in history had withered away?" We then read of the greatness of Greece and of Rome; of the glories of Egypt and Persia: but all of them had become museum-pieces. On the other hand, how was it that the vitality of Indian Culture had continued through the ages despite historical vicissitudes? Why?[13]

Munshi essentially saw culture as a continuity:

> A culture becomes a flowing stream only when there is continuity of collective life in a people. In other words, a distinctive culture comes into existence when a people develop a continuous way of life. Such continuity expresses itself in various ways; in common traditions and norms of conduct; in common institutions; in a common memory of

12 K.M. Munshi, *Foundations of Indian Culture*, 1974, p. 2.

13 Ibid., pp. 1-2.

> triumphs achieved; in a common aesthetic outlook; in a capacity for characteristic collective action.[14]

His principal concern was for this continuity to be preserved and carried forward by being handed over to future generations. For him this signified fundamentally the reintegration of Indian culture under modern conditions and every regenerative cultural activity that he undertook in his lifetime had this as its central objective. In later years, Munshi talked of the need for an active "dominant minority". A minority which would ensure this vital cultural continuity and flow, he saw it as the only safeguard against the "dangers of disintegration".[15] It was this "dominant minority" which for him had to recapture the "values of a culture" for each generation "by a subtle process of reinterpretation, reintegration and adaptation".[16] The danger of a second-hand existence though, Munshi warned, was acute and could worsen:

> Suppose a time comes in India God forbid – when our young men and women are lost to the values and ideals of our culture, our culture would be dead. Then they may become civilized barbarians or second-class Westerners, but they can never be the torch-bearers of a living Indian culture for the age in which they live or for the future.[17]

In his lifetime and through his work, Munshi did much to work for that "reinterpretation, reintegration and adaptation". Sadly his contributions and interventions which did much to highlight the centrality of culture in the national life of independent India remain today woefully unacknowledged and marginalized.

---

14 K.M. Munshi, *Foundations of Indian Culture,* 1974, p. 4.

15 Ibid., p. 9.

16 Ibid.

17 Ibid., p. 10.

7

Syama Prasad Mookerjee
Reforging India's Cultural Links

In trying to widen the discussion it is interesting to read of the approach to culture of another public personality who was intimately associated for a period with education in the country and in independent India's first parliament went on to coalesce the first democratic opposition. There is not much that Syama Prasad Mookerjee (1901-53), has left behind in terms of cultural writings and thought, but a survey of his papers do help in creating an assessment of his deep cultural propensities.

As one of the youngest vice-chancellors of the University of Calcutta between 1934 and 1938, Mookerjee encouraged the founding of the Asutosh Museum of Indian Art, the first public museum to be established in any university in India. His father, Sir Asutosh Mookerjee, the legendary vice-chancellor of the same university had inaugurated earlier a new phase in research on Indian history and culture by supporting a number of young Indian scholars.[1] The Department of Ancient Indian History and Culture was thus

---

1 In a letter to E.B. Havell, Abanindranath Tagore, discussed the state of art and cultural training in the University of Calcutta and of how Asutosh Mookerjee did much to generate a comprehensive momentum towards a real study of Indian culture. He also lamented that the "sad and untimely death" of Asutosh Mookerjee had "to a great extent retarded the art work in the University. He was the →

launched and at a time when the *swadeshi*-inspired national education movement was collapsing Asutosh's reformist zeal at the University captivated and reoriented a number of promising young minds who, while plunging into the study of Indian culture and history that the University facilitated, could still hold on to and strengthen their nationalist credentials without fear of official repression. Syama Prasad continued to strengthen that tradition by actively expanding the profile and horizon of the university in the areas of Indian cultural and historical studies.

in 1945, as president of the Council of Post Graduate teaching in Arts of the university Syama Prasad welcomed collaboration with nationalist China in expanding the university's reach. Welcoming a proposal by the then Chinese minister of education of a scholarship grant for teaching Chinese to Indian students in Calcutta, Mookerjee also impressed upon the Chinese to depute to his university their scholars who would undertake rigorous study of Indian culture and civilization:

> It is . . . desirable that a Chinese scholar should come out to Calcutta to stay here for a year or two. . . . In this connection I may state for your information that the University has received an endowment from one of its alumni, the object of which is to enable the University to invite some foreign scholars to spend a year or two in Calcutta and work on some subject connected with Hindu culture and civilization. . . . You may select some distinguished scholars who may be anxious to receive training in Sanskrit or Indian philosophy

→ prime mover and my great supporter and was building the foundation of great University when he was suddenly taken away." Then referring to Syama Prasad, Abanindranath consoled himself, "However I find that one of his sons is taking interest in art and a number of M.A. students are beginning to see the usefulness of art line. So I have every hope for the future." (Cited in S.P. Basu, *Nivedita Lokmata*, vol. 4, p. 85.)

> or Indian history or any other subject connected with our culture and civilization and depute him to remain here for a year or two. . . .[2]

Mookerjee also followed up the matter with Chiang-Kai-Shek himself and thanked the "Generalissimo" for the policies of his government that have enabled the growth of "close cultural contacts between China and the University of Calcutta".[3]

Post-Independence, Mookerjee realized the need for India to try and reforge her civilizational-cultural linkages with her South-East Asian neighbours. As president of the Mahabodhi Society from 1949, he personally undertook to relay and revive these cultural links. His cultural activism during this period reflected his concern that India's ancient neighbours be made to feel again a part of India's ancient civilizational legacy without imparting a hegemonistic hue to the entire effort. Mookerjee was instrumental in arranging as a "permanent loan" a portion of the sacred relics of the two chief disciples of the Buddha for the Burmese by deftly negotiating the matter between the Burmese and Indian governments. In a letter to Nehru, Mookerjee explained the effects that the relics of the Buddha had on the people of that country and the need to give a careful consideration to their request of being given a portion of it. The Prime Minister of Burma, Thakin Nu (U Nu) had himself made the request to Syama Prasad while he crossed Calcutta some time in the early part of 1950.

> . . . I met the prime minister of Burma while he was passing through Calcutta on his way to England a few weeks ago. He is anxious to obtain from the Mahabodhi Society a small portion of the sacred relics of Buddha to be enshrined in

---

2 Syama Prasad Mookerjee's letter dated 5 October 1945 to Chu-Chia-Hua, minister of education, Chinese Government, Chungking.

3 Syama Prasad Mookerjee's letter dated 5 October 1945 to Chiang-Kai-Shek.

> Rangoon. Some time ago [February-April 1950], the Mahabodhi Society took some of the sacred relics to Burma and they evoked widespread feelings of enthusiasm and reverence throughout Burma. The Prime Minister of Burma is anxious that a small portion of the relics may be kept in Burma. This will have a unifying influence on the people of Burma and will also establish good feelings between India and Burma. . . .[4]

In another letter to S. Dutt, then Secretary in the Ministry of External Affairs, Mookerjee explained his reasons for trying to push this through:

> By allowing portions of the relics to be kept in Burma, we will be forging another close link between India and Burma in religious and cultural spheres, which, I have no doubt,

[4] Syama Prasad Mookerjee's letter to Pandit Nehru dated 19 May 1950. The relics were taken to Burma on invitation from the Government of Burma in early 1950, U Nu flew down to Calcutta to receive the relics and "after a 2½ months stay in Burma the relics were brought back on 16 April" (*Annual Report of the Mahabodhi Society of India* for 1950). Interestingly, some time later, on 14 June 1950, U Win, then Burmese education minister and acting foreign minister in his presidential address at an event organized by the Cultural Studies Group of the Ramakrishna Mission Society at Rangoon, spoke on "The Need for Indo-Burman Cultural Contacts". Win referred to India as the "one country with which Burma has most contact throughout history" and called for closer co-operation between the two. A closer relation with Burma, Win said would help India play her rightful role in South-East Asian affairs, "History has shown that India and Burma must march together in amity and concord if they were to achieve greatness in accordance with the direction of Nature. We know each other as few people do. Our understanding of each other's needs and difficulties is very profound and deep-rooted. With such knowledge and understanding, sympathy is not difficult of cultivation." U Win concluded that in the future, India and Burma "are going to play very important parts" and both had much to give to the "new Asia". And Burma, "owing to her deep understanding of India through long association and her racial affinity with the people →

> will have good effect on Indo–Burmese relationship generally.[5]

Realizing the great potential for cultural outreach that the occasion held, Mookerjee with great initiative finally saw the process through by convincing the Indian Prime Minister. It was decided that portions of the relics of Buddha's chief disciples – Sariputta and Moggallana – would be given to Burma as "permanent loans". To U Nu Mookerjee wrote that he had "every hope that this will strengthen still further the bonds of union between India and Burma and bring peace and contentment to peoples of your great country".[6] For the people of Burma, then in a civil war situation with various factions of communists trying to gain control of the newly-independent country such a move was symbolic of a spiritual-cultural solace. In a letter, expressing his gratitude to Mookerjee "on behalf of the government and the people of Burma" U Nu expressed his confidence that this "noble and generous gift of some portions of the sacred relics of the *arahant*s Sariputta and Moggallana for permanent enshrinement in Burma" would:

> further cement the already very close and unique relationship between our two sister countries. . . . The whole of the Buddhist world, I am sure, would join me in saying "*sadhu*! *sadhu*! *sadhu*!" for the noble gesture and meritorious deed of your good-self and the Mahabodhi Society of India.[7]

→ of South-East Asia, [was] in an ideal position as a bridge between India and South-East Asian countries". (U Win, "The Need for Indo-Burman Cultural Contacts" in *The Vedanta Kesari*, vol. XXXVII, no. 6, October 1950, pp. 222-23.)

5 Syama Prasad Mookerjee's letter, dated 18 November 1950.

6 Syama Prasad Mookerjee's letter, dated 30 November 1950.

7 Thakin Nu's letter dated 27 November 1950. India's "permanent loan" of the Relics created a great stir in Burma. On 21 January 1951 a "specially chartered plane" flew the Relics to Rangoon. After travelling all over the country the Relics were finally enshrined at the →

fig. 7: Syama Prasad Mookerjee with Nehru and Thakin Nu, Calcutta, 1949

fig. 8: Syama Prasad Mookerjee handing over the sacred relics to Thakin Nu, 1950

In August 1952 Mookerjee wrote to the foreign minister of Cambodia that he was looking forward to visiting that ancient country and to "renewing the old bonds between our country and yours. Lord Buddha is a mighty connecting link between India and many other countries in the world today".[8] He visited Cambodia carrying the relics and seems to have made a wide impact. One of his biographers writes that "over a million monks and laymen lined the route from the aerodrome to the Silver Pagoda where the relics were to be kept for worship". Mookerjee later addressed a crowd of about half a million in the main square of the city on the message of the Buddha and "the cultural ties between India and the Buddhist countries".[9] At Saigon and Bangkok similar scenes were seen and an outpouring of goodwill and attraction for India and her culture was witnessed by the delegation.[10]

In November 1952 Mookerjee helped conceptualize and organize a grand international cultural conference on the occasion of the inauguration of the new *vihara* at Sanchi where the other portion of the relics of the two chief disciples were to be reinterred. He used the occasion to reitrate the necessity of re-creating India–South-East Asia cultural bonds. In his welcome address at the inaugural session of this mega cultural conference presided over by S. Radhakrishnan, then Vice-President of India, Mookerjee articulated his vision:

> Many of these countries in S.E. Asia after attaining independence are striving hard to receive the highest elements

→ Kaba Aye Pagoda in early March 1952, Syama Prasad was a specially invited guest on the occasion. (For a detailed study see e.g. Jack Daulton, "Sariputta and Moggallana in the Golden Land" in *The Journal of Burma Studies*, vol. 4, 1999, pp. 100-28.)

[8] Syama Prasad Mookerjee's letter dated 21 August 1952.

[9] Balraj Madhok, *Dr. Syama Prasad Mookerjee: A Biography*, 1954, p. 189.

[10] Ibid., p. 190.

> of Buddhist cultural and religious thought. In this respect India occupies the role of their spiritual mother. . . . With a true sense of humility and responsibility India can re-establish the bonds of friendship and understanding with them so that this fraternity will not only be welcomed by the peoples of the countries concerned but will also create a mighty source of strength and solidarity which can worthily contribute to the maintenance of world peace and freedom.[11]

At the inauguration of the new *vihara* the next day Mookerjee spoke on the role of such cultural centres as Sanchi, "Such centres must not remain confined to the educated few", he observed, "from them must flow currents of thought and service" for the benefit of the people to develop in them a quest for culture, and for the preservation of Indian culture and her symbols.[12]

Syama Prasad Mookerjee, essentially a consistent advocate for developing hard power and national strength, also clearly saw the need to evolve a cultural approach that would reinvent India's civilizational ties with her neighbours essentially inspired by the *svabhava* of a spiritual mother and not a cultural hegemon. His biographer also notes that during his brief stop over at the Bangkok Airport having witnessed the overwhelming response of the people Mookerjee was surprised to learn from Indian officials that such events were rarely reported back to India.[13] Clearly in the sphere of culture Indian diplomacy in this region had a head-start over her larger neighbour but such an advantage was never effectively put into use and opportunities were allowed to be squandered away. This explains why even in 2011 the project for the restoration and development of Lumbini in Nepal finds expression and

---

11 Balraj Madhok, *Dr. Syama Prasad Mookerjee: A Biography*, 1954, p. 191.

12 Ibid.

13 Ibid., p. 190.

fig. 9: Syama Prasad Mookerjee rediscovering India's cultural footprints in Cambodia, 1952. Courtesy: www.shamaprasad.org

support from China while India flounders and ignores the entire issue.[14] A defined vision that would preserve and rejuvenate our ancient cultural centres and evolve newer ones by spreading the ideals of Indian civilization and culture were never really considered in great earnestness.

Mookerjee's contribution and activism in the cultural sphere may have been overshadowed by his political action but it nevertheless serves as a reminder that culture was to him one of the central pillars of the new republic and of its effort at restating its civilizational identity.

---

[14] In 2011 the Chinese organization "Asia Pacific Exchange and Cooperation Foundation" (APECF) announced an investment of up to USD 3 billion to build a "special development zone" in Nepal by transforming the town of Lumbini into "a mega tourist, pilgrim and education centre" and evolve it as a "strategic centre for promoting Buddhist culture". The project received the backing of the Chinese government at the highest levels and aimed to unite all three strands of Buddhism including the Tibetan. The Nepalese cultural ministry was not taken into confidence over the entire proposal. Though the lid seems to have been shut for the time being over the project it only showed how proactive the Chinese establishment had become in trying to forge China's cultural ties with its neighbours. Apart from its cultural aspect the project has wide ramifications for India's security as well. The Indian government has hardly ever shown interest in the project, despite, Nehru's exhortation that the spot of Lumbini be included in plans that India had of developing a Buddhist pilgrim circuit. (For a detailed analysis of the Lumbini project see e.g. my "Encircling the 'Light of Asia': The Lumbini Project", VIF Paper, 8 August 2011 at: http://www.vifindia.org/article/2011/august/08/Encircling-the%20-Light-of-Asia-the-Lumbini-Project.)

8

Jawaharlal Nehru
India's Culture and Her National Life

DESPITE his opposition to any effort undertaken along similar lines as the one at Somanatha, Nehru, to his credit, did display a wide understanding of the need to work actively in the area of culture and contributed his bit by trying to create an approach to the issue of culture in independent India. He could, however, never really develop a firm foundation for a serious relook at culture in independent India nor develop a much needed recognition of the centrality of culture in our national life. It was perhaps too difficult and intricate a task for one mind to accomplish, nevertheless Nehru tried to generate a certain degree of awareness nationally on culture.

Nehru seemed to have realized early, the necessity of re-projecting India's culture beyond her shores and of developing an active national plan for cultural education and rejuvenation. Thus, in spite of the huge pressures of the times, the first decade after Independence saw efforts made at creating cultural institutions with the hope of ushering in a new era of cultural and aesthetic education and growth. As early as April 1950, Nehru clearly stated this point when he said in his inaugural address of the Indian Council of Cultural Relations (ICCR) that he had "always looked forward to furthering the cause of India's cultural association, not only with the neighbouring countries to the East and West but with the wider world outside". For him it was

> not a question of merely wanting such a cultural association or considering it good; it [was] rather a question of the necessity of the situation which is bound to worsen if nothing is done to prevent it. . . .[1]

A premier institution of the arts and letters, the Sahitya Akademi was inaugurated on 12 March 1954 with the object of setting "high literary standards" and co-ordinating "literary activities in all Indian languages". It was also expected to promote "cultural exchange with other countries and maintain liaison with international cultural organizations". Nehru, who envisaged the project, had a grand plan for the entire initiative. In a note written days before the inauguration he argued that it was not good enough for the Sahitya Akademi "to be merely a co-ordinating agency. . . ." The vision rather, was to make it, "something like the French Academy or its British counterpart" and for this its "scope [had] to be enlarged . . . [so that it became] a much more important body than a co-ordinating agency. . . ."[2]

Initiative was taken in the 1950s to design and create some of the principal establishments of Indian culture and these efforts were undertaken simultaneously with the creation of other state infrastructures and were seen to be essential for the growth of an integral national life. Discussing the preservation of Indian historic sites and their art, Nehru called for developing these as "places of artistic pilgrimage" so that a sustained exposure would eventually have a positive effect on the collective life:

> The type of great art we have has essentially to be seen on the site itself . . . it is part of the natural scene like some of our great sculptures, caves and frescoes. It is right that these places should become, even more so than they are now, places of

[1] Extract from Nehru's inaugural address at the Indian Council of Cultural Relations (ICCR), 9 April 1950, New Delhi.

[2] Prime Minister's note to B.M. Kaul, Principal Private Secretary, dated 9 March 1954.

> artistic pilgrimage for us so that we may learn from them not only something of the past but some thing of the grace of life which can, perhaps, affect our present life also.[3]

Referring to the role of museums and describing their actual functioning, Nehru again defined the parameters:

> . . . A museum which is really meant to interest and educate must be something which connects its objects with the things the visitors are used to seeing in their lives and in their environments. It should not be just a symbol of the distant, unconnected past. I do not know how far our experts think on these lines. . . . The whole point of museums, whether they be museums of antiquity or museums of modern life, is that larger and larger numbers of people visit them and learn from them. . . . More and more people should come and learn and, in fact, facilities for learning should be provided . . . some arrangements should be made for lectures to be given to ordinary folk who come there and for guides to explain to them what these things are and arouse their interest in them, especially school children and college boys and girls. . . .[4]

It was vital that the aspect of "education through the museums be developed", Nehru saw them as central to the education of the nation:

> . . . every child of India should see something of [the] artistic treasures, should understand something that has gone to build up India, should assimilate, even if in a small measure, the genius of India, which, adapted to the modern conditions, should make the country grow.[5]

---

3 Speech at the inauguration of the National Art Treasures Fund, New Delhi, 23 February 1952.

4 Speech at the Centenary Celebrations of the Madras Government Museum and the opening the National Art Gallery, Madras, 27 November 1951.

5 Speech at the inauguration of the National Art Treasures Fund, New Delhi, 23 February 1952.

Interestingly he also cautioned against any tendency to turn the museum into just another routine government body meant only for classification and storage work. He wanted these bodies to thrive with life and act as crucial and attractive bridges between India's past and her present. Referring to the standard attitude in a government museum Nehru perhaps anticipated what was to come:

> . . . It is not interested in the public seeing the exhibits; it is interested in ticketing and docketing and presenting a report at the end . . . that may have some value for the future. But certainly the value it has in the present is practically nil, because the museum [then does not become] a part of the life of the people but merely of the officials who sit there. The whole idea of museums [then] somehow seems to be unconnected with the life of our people. It lives in the upper atmosphere of officials. That is not good enough and the question arises how we can make museums a vital part of our people's lives.[6]

For a hugely burdened first Prime Minister of a newly independent nation Nehru displayed a remarkable sensitivity towards the physical preservation of our past. His meticulous note to the Governor and Premier of Orissa for the preservation of the Konark Temple displays his concern for these mighty symbols of Indian culture:

1. Two days ago I visited the Konark Temple and spent some hours there in the company of His Excellency the Governor and the Premier of Orissa. This temple is a magnificent structure, unique in many ways. It deserves preservation.
2. I found many pieces of stones and rock lying about all round the temple. Many of these pieces were of value

[6] Speech at the inauguration of the National Art Treasures Fund, New Delhi, 23 February 1952.

and should have been separated and kept apart in some kind of museum or at least a shed. There was a small museum where some important pieces of sculpture had been arranged. But much more could have been done and should be done. As it is, there is a grave danger of our losing some valuable specimens. Indeed I was told that people took away many of these pieces, either as souvenirs or for some other purpose.

3. I do not know what the Archaeological Department is doing in this matter. Of course, what will ultimately be necessary is large-scale excavation all around. This may wait awhile owing to financial stringency. But I think something should be done immediately. There is always the danger of the parts of the temple collapsing. I suggest that the following steps be taken:
   (i) A very close survey of the temple and the pieces of stone and sculpture lying about. All the worthwhile pieces should be separated and put in a proper shed.
   (ii) Photographs of the temple and its separate parts and important sculptures should be taken in some profusion and a record made. A small cinema film might also be made and it may be desirable to issue a small illustrated booklet on the Konark Temple.
4. All this has to be done by some competent archaeologist from the centre who should have the help and co-operation of the provincial government.[7]

Feeling the need to develop, revive and strengthen a shared cultural past Nehru argued in 1955 for the need to develop the Buddhist holy sites in India and in the

[7] Note to the Governor and Premier of Orissa, 12 March 1949, File No. 7(74)/48-PMS.

neighbourhood in active collaboration with the people and government of those countries. He had realized the necessity of reinventing shared civilizational linkages in the region and in this context the need to develop Lumbini, found mention even then. In a note on the development and conservation of these sacred places Nehru envisioned the drawing up of a comprehensive and far-seeing plan with this aim in mind:

> I suggest that we should undertake the task of improving in every way the places in India connected with the Buddha. This would include Bodh-Gaya, Kushinara, Sarnath, Lumbini, Rajgir. Possibly there are some more. In Sanchi something has already been done. . . . Lumbini has been completely neglected and even the roads are not good. The prime minister of Burma has suggested that a kind of park should be made at Lumbini with certain buildings. I suggest that we might send an engineer and an architect to visit these places and to make recommendations as to what should be done.[8]

Towards the end of May 1955, when the question of forming the Bodh-Gaya Temple Committee cropped up, an effort was made to utilize the opportunity to develop a greater cultural–religious partnership with countries that had a sizeable Buddhist population. The aim was to reactivate some of the major Indian civilizational anchors and through them to reach out to the wide world, especially to civilizations that once shared close links and which could again form part of a larger cultural coalition. Nehru indicated the broader objective of the temple committee formation. The main purpose of the advisory board of the temple was "to bring in foreign representatives from Buddhist countries", he wrote:

---

8 Note of 10 April 1955. In an earlier note dated 27 March 1955 to the Secretary, Ministry of Education, Nehru referred to the need to develop supporting infrastructure in these sacred sites and mentions the lack of approach roads at Lumbini.

> The whole idea is to make this advisory board rather an international body . . . and we have to give a sense of partnership to the foreign countries. . . . I would suggest the following [foreign representations]:
>
> Burma: 2; Ceylon: 2; Nepal: 1; Tibet: 1; Thailand: 1; Cambodia: 1; Laos: 1; Japan: 1
>
> These are the principal Buddhist countries. Indonesia has practically no Buddhist population or, at any rate, a very small one. China has many Buddhists and I would not mind if China (apart from Tibet) was also invited to send one. But I would not suggest this to begin with. This gives you ten numbers. I have indicated two for both Burma and Ceylon because both have a far greater interest in Bodh-Gaya than any of the more distant countries. . . . We must remember that this advisory body will have a larger significance than merely one for the Bodh-Gaya Temple. It really brings India into the international picture from another point of view.[9]

But for this entire exercise to take shape and deliver results a national awareness had to be first regenerated and created *vis-à-vis* Indian culture and the physical manifestations of her culture nationally and worldwide.

Despite all this envisioning, the rediscovering of external cultural linkages and through them the immense potential to develop a renewed Indian cultural reach, especially in the South-East Asian region, has been largely overlooked while developing cultural policies and schemes over the years. Such a

---

[9] Letter dated 25 May 1955 to the then chief minister of Bihar Sri Krishna Sinha (Sri Babu) (1887–1961). It is perhaps another matter altogether that the project of reconstructing the ancient university at Nalanda which began sometime in 2007 has completely kept out Tibetan representation and has either marginalized or relegated to the periphery the other nations mentioned in Nehru's list. Ironically the project has allowed a single country, China, with a past history of Buddhist persecution, to wield an inordinate influence over the entire scheme of things.

laissez faire approach has only allowed China the space to build itself up as the official arbiter of cultural and religious affairs – particularly of Buddhism – in the region.[10]

There is however, no comprehensive or single answer as to why Nehru, himself culturally conscious, having envisioned the creation of cultural academies and institutions could never really thrust forward with India's cultural power – within the country and beyond. Externally, for example, despite his professed understanding of the currents of international diplomacy and cultural relations, Nehru did not appear to have paid sufficient attention in terms of culture, towards South-East Asia – the region closest to India geographically and culturally. It is said that the selection of ambassadors who were sent to countries in this region, then, was "often done with little care; and, not infrequently, the wrong type of person [represented] India". These were persons who were usually "supercilious and West-oriented", and were "always resentful of having been sent to an under-developed country".[11]

---

10 Displaying its adverse stand on the "Global Buddhist Congregation" which saw the congregation of 800 scholars from over thirty-two countries in New Delhi in November 2011, China attempted to generate pressure on the organizers as well the Government of India to prevent H.H. the Dalai Lama from addressing the gathering. ("China Opposes Countries 'Providing Platform' to Dalai Lama", *Hindustan Times*, 28 November 2011, Ananth Krishnan "China Warns India Against 'providing platform' for Dalai Lama", *The Hindu*, 28 November 2011.)

11 Amiya Rao, B.G. Rao, *Six Thousand Days*, 1974, p. 221. This cultural distance between India under Nehru and this region is best illustrated by the following account of what happened when the first Indian ambassador to one of these countries landed. His announced arrival had caused "considerable interest and expectation" and delegations of Hindu and Buddhist priests had arrived at the airport with "flowers, conch-shells and drums to welcome the representative of the country that had given them their Scriptures". To the consternation of those assembled, "the ambassador emerged pipe in mouth, fully accoutred →

Of the twenty regular publicity posts then maintained abroad by the Indian Ministry of External Affairs, only three were allotted to this vast region.[12] No efforts were initiated to "bring this area nearer to India" in cultural terms by "arranging to teach any of its languages in any of the Indian universities or founding chairs in Indian languages in any of their universities". While senior ministers and officers of the Indian government and delegations of legislators preferred "the more affluent capitals of the world", few made any effort to go to Saigon, Hanoi, Pnom Penh, Vientiane, Rangoon. In his entire seventeen-years tenure, Nehru, visited North Vietnam, South Vietnam and Cambodia only once, and relegated Laos to the periphery, "he made only a brief three-hour stop-over at Vientiane in 1954".[13] It is hard to explain Nehru's apathy towards these culturally rich and alive countries and their people given that in his *The Discovery of India,* he had devoted much space and analysis to the "Indian Colonies and Culture in South-East Asia". He appeared to be fully aware of the civilizational and cultural import of the region when he passionately wrote, "Indian civilization took root especially in the countries of South-East Asia and the evidence for this can be found all over the place today. There

→ in Western clothes, a brown sahib". The gathering rapidly dissipated, "their flowers unshowered, their conches unblown, their drums unbeaten" (ibid., p. 221).

12 *Six Thousand Days*, p. 221. Indian policy in south-east during these years suffered "the loss of power and prestige and a draining away of accumulated capital of goodwill mostly because of its poor diplomacy". In South-East Asia it appeared to be "devoid of all tact and imagination". During this long period India professed "Asian solidarity but [her] diplomatic attention was principally focused on Europe". (D.P. Singhal, "Indian Policy in South-East Asia" in *Nationalism in India and Other Historical Essays*, 1967, p. 310.)

13 *Six Thousand Days*, pp. 221-22.

were great centres of Sanskrit learning in Champa, Angkor, Srivijaya, Majapahit, and other places. The names of the rulers of the various states and empires that arose are purely Indian and Sanskrit. This does not mean that they were pure Indian, but it does mean that they were Indianized. . . ." Approvingly citing a letter he had received from a Thai student who had come to study at Tagore's Santiniketan and who wrote of how fortunate he was to pay his humble homage at the "feet of grandmother India in whose affectionate arms" his "mother country was so lovingly brought up and taught to appreciate and love what was sublime and beautiful in culture and religion", Nehru concluded that it pointed to the continued existence of some "general feeling towards India which, though vague and overladen with much else, still continues in many of the countries of South-East Asia". Behind all vicissitudes, he saw persisting in this region, "a feeling of respect and friendship for India, for old memories endure and people have not forgotten that there was a time when India was a mother country to these and nourished them with rich fare from her own treasure house".[14] And yet in his long and uninterrupted tenure as Prime Minister, Nehru seemed to have strangely allowed this very memory and feeling to dilute and to eventually subside. The areas that once held the "most famous two Hindu kingdoms of Indo-China", Champa and Khmer and were "thoroughly saturated with Indian culture"[15] remained neglected.

---

14 Jawaharlal Nehru, *The Discovery of India*, 1985, pp. 207-09.

15 D.P. Singhal, "Indian Contribution to Human Civilisation" in *Nationalism in India*, p. 174. This happened despite the people of the area and their leaders acknowledging with great reverence that India was for them "what Greece was for the Latin Occident". (Late King Norodom Sihanouk's observations at the inauguration of a grand boulevard in memory of Nehru at Phnom Penh in 1965, D.P. Singhal, *India and World Civilisation*, vol. 2, 1969, pp. 133-32.)

In fact, in a letter to the Prime Minister of Sri Lanka in 1953, Nehru surprisingly wrote, "As for Asian unity, such unity has to be based on some common understanding and common objectives. I see little in common". Though he left no opportunity to "[romanticize] the spirit of Asia" he did "little to promote such common understanding and common objective".[16] Especially in the cultural field such initiative was sorely lacking, India, under Nehru, forgot to "re-enact the feeling of oneness"[17] with the countries of this region – and displayed the absence of a strategic cultural vision.

The effects of the absence of such a cultural vision are felt to this day, when a neglected ICCR, India's premier body for cultural diplomacy and outreach, continues to cry for greater support and faces constraints in fulfilling its external mandate[18] while the budgetary allocations for culture for the year 2012-13 has been whittled down to one-third of the amount requested by the Union Ministry of Culture.

The May 2012 report of the Parliamentary Standing Committee on Culture has pointed to this strange state of affairs where the Government of India has decided to allocate

---

16 *Six Thousand Days*, p. 222.

17 Singhal, *Indian Policy in South-East Asia*, p. 313.

18 For example the 2012-13 budget for the ICCR has been kept at the same as for the year 2011-12. This has been done at a time when ICCR is expanding its cultural outreach activities in the country as well as abroad and is repeatedly asking for an enhanced budgetary allocation. The Parliamentary Standing Committee on External Affairs in its Report on Demands for Grants (2012-13) drew attention to this stagnation in resource allocation for the ICCR while observing that "during the last three years the ICCR has been allocated almost the same fund of Rs. 150 crore against their demand ranging from Rs. 166 to 225 crore this year". The Committee starkly remarked that with "such insufficient fund allocation ICCR will not be able to achieve the objectives of cultural diplomacy with any meaningful impact".

against a demand of Rs. 2,916.43 crore an amount of only Rs. 864 crore for 2012-13 for culture. The committee was surprised to note the "apathy of the government towards the cause of preservation and promotion of our ancient culture". During the previous plan – the Eleventh Five Year Plan – the total allocation for culture amounted to a share of just 0.16 per cent of the total central plan allocation of the Government of India. This is certainly indefensible especially when one looks at India's vast cultural diversities and richness and the acute need for preserving and revivifying a number of her cultural and historical symbols. The Parliamentary Committee observed that the Ministry of Culture "certainly deserves a better treatment in allocation of funds in view of its importance" and called upon the nodal disbursing units of the state such as the Union Ministry of Finance and the Central Planning Commission to appreciate this fact and to display a greater sensitivity while allocating funds for culture.

Had Nehru, propelled by his concern for the state of culture in the country, really layed the foundation of a solid framework for the preservation and dissemination of culture in India such a situation would perhaps have never arisen in the first place. Had India's first Prime Minister really laid the foundation for cultural research in the country, had he through the force of his personality, intellect, keen understanding of Indian culture reignited the debate on culture, one would have surely seen a greater awareness and aspiration in our national life towards studying, appreciating and absorbing the fundamentals of Indian culture. Its deeper symbolism would have then permeated our quotidian life and kept alive and pulsating the many cultural manifestations of India and her people.

It is not to argue that Nehru did not do enough under the prevailing situation in the country, he did lay a certain foundation, but he failed to generate a robust and accommodating debate on the essentials of Indian culture and of its role and position in our national life and education. In short, in his years in power Nehru was unsuccessful in initiating a rediscovery of India and especially in nurturing and supporting the "old Indian cultural tradition"[19] that had so attracted him during his earlier discovery of his country and her people.

[19] *The Discovery of India*, p. 58.

9

Culture : The Continuing Debate

THE *tour d'horizon* of the debate on Indian culture has revealed an intricate and multifaceted dialogue and engagement with the issue. Apart from the fascinating dimensions of these debates and formulations on culture what strikes one is the fact that some of these thought leaders, despite a multitude of absorbing interests and preoccupations never seemed to have ceased to be fascinated by Indian culture. Their interest was not superficial and arising out of a shallow curiosity or the manifestations of a very modern affliction called "time-pass", but was a deep and abiding one. So intense was this interest, that it led most of them to reflect deeply not only on contemporary cultural issues but to also dwell on the future of Indian culture and on its continuity in future India's national life.[1] Most of them believed that an independent India would carry forward their concern for its culture and give it a certain centrality in its scheme of things. The national mind, they believed, once awakened to the light of its culture would ceaselessly find interest and nourishment from its inspiring principles and manifestations. They seem to have believed that India, which had been a "beautiful country not so long

[1] We have chosen our thinkers from one particular category, they are those , to use a phrase from Sri Aurobindo, who have studied Indian culture with the "eye of sympathy and intuition and a close appreciative self-identification". (Sri Aurobindo "A Rationalistic Critic of Indian Culture", *CWSA*, vol. 20, p. 97.)

ago" would again move forward in reclaiming that cultural height. Such a belief made them talk of restoring the consciousness towards beauty among the people of India.

Our thinkers were also concerned about Indian culture in the world – a world which was progressively growing closer and in which they saw imperial powers acting as cultural hegemons. They resisted all efforts to impose a cultural homogeneity and vigorously challenged any attempts at cultural hegemony. Their self-imposed mission at hand was to awaken an Indian interest in India, an Indian thirst for the re-examination of Indian culture and to help evolve an Indian image of Indian culture. And yet, such a conviction did not seem to have narrowed their cultural horizon. They were open to the world, welcomed its myriad cultures and ways of life and enthusiastically sought to examine them, while assiduously scrutinizing their adaptability to the Indian context and milieu.

Interestingly, these thinkers had wide exposure to the West and quite early developed the habit of comparing cultures and civilizations. While marvelling at India's world-reach in a past epoch they saw the need to reclaim or at least to reactivate that cultural outreach under present conditions. At the same time they were disturbed at the Indian mind's apathy towards its own cultural foundations. They deplored in an articulate section of Indians, the tendency of neglecting the cultural continuum and the propensity of seconding all interpretations of India which emerged from Western readings. In any case, the Western education that they benefited from in the West, these thinkers saw as being misapplied to the Indian context and of serving to dry up the Indian mind's interests in a true reading of its cultural past and future.

My reading of these thinkers convinced me that they held the hope that an India free to determine its destiny would give a place of importance to the study of Indian culture and to the dissemination of its cultural principles. They believed that this would happen with young minds being introduced to the wonders of their culture and with the unleashing in them of a fascination for Indian culture. But perhaps they were too trusting of the future; perhaps they were too simplistic in their reading of the future cultural enthusiasm of the nation and failed to see, or could not imagine, that in a free India culture would find it difficult to expand its base in a society that would gradually be dominated by politics and commerce. The predominance of the utilitarian motive would overshadow the epochal role and concern for culture and to see it happening in India would have particularly disturbed and puzzled them.

Neglect of culture by official India and neglect of culture in Indian education are two issues that repeatedly come to the fore. In fact, details of such neglect is symptomatic of a continuing general apathy for culture in India and is demonstrative of the confusion that prevails on the need to understand, study and project Indian culture. It would suffice to make a brief survey of the educational and the official neglect of culture in India and show how we have succeeded in relegating culture to the periphery of our national life. We have quietly ignored the fact that in spite of their often precarious existence and fighting against a dominant and powerful group which sought to impose a prejudiced reading of India, our cultural nationalists held fort and strove hard to generate a counter-opinion and evolve a counter-narrative where perceptions and issues of culture dominated. We have allowed that debate to rest by ignoring culture.

Starving Culture: Officially

That there exists an acute official neglect of culture in India is evident from official documents and testimonies. A look at the Parliamentary Standing Committee Report on the Ministry of Culture for 2012-13 will reveal this official apathy which has afflicted cultural efforts for years together. The apathy is most visible in the state of our cultural symbols and repositories. Apart from a reduced funding, the expenditure – the Parliamentary Committee noted – was "less in those areas which are critical for preservation and propagation of culture and invariably require more funds such as the ASI [Archaeological Survey of India], Museums and archives".[2] These bodies which ought to have been continuously encouraged to reinvent themselves and nationally spearhead cultural research and study while working towards re-creating India's historical and cultural links worldwide continue to suffer from a great shortage of manpower and expertise. The Committee noted this point when it underlined the "huge gap between the sanctioned strength and assessed strength, almost in all categories of staff and officers". Such a state, it argued, was "certainly telling upon the work relating to preservation and protection" of monuments[3] and also on further research, excavation and dissemination.

Regarding the state of one of the premier national repositories of Indian culture, the Committee's observations are worth noting and are disturbing as well. On the state of the National Museum in New Delhi, right under the watchful eyes of officialdom, the Committee found that it was "not being properly managed". It noted that at least in this case there was no dearth of funds but the attitude pointed to the general apathy that has percolated into most of our cultural institutions. The reasons for the museum's malfunctioning, the Committee pointed out, were the "large number of posts lying vacant for years, lack of personnel with required training-skill, poor upkeep-maintenance, galleries being closed for longer periods"

---

[2] *One Hundred Seventy Fifth Report on Demands for Grants (2012-13) of Ministry of Culture*, May 2012 (henceforth *Demands for Grants*).

[3] *Demands for Grants*, para 35.

and a "lack of co-ordination with other agencies".[4] If such is the case with the premier National Museum, one can imagine the state of other lesser known museums all over the country.

On the display of objects in the National Museum, the Committee highlighted the prevailing apathy as well. It is a far cry from the vision that Nehru nurtured of museums in India. Coomaraswamy, once discussing the exhibiting of objects in museums had dwelt on their meaning, need and methodology. It is interesting to read parts of it and to realize how that vision has been totally omitted from our considerations today. In an essay, "Why Exhibit Works of Art", Coomaraswamy discussed the entire pattern and reason of display in museums, when he wrote:

> If we are to exhibit these objects for educational reasons, and not as mere curios, it is evident that we are proposing to make such use of them as is possible without an actual handling. It will be imaginatively and not actually that we must use the mediaeval reliquary, or lie on the Egyptian bed, or make our offering to some ancient deity. The educational ends that an exhibition can serve demand, accordingly, the services not of a Curator only, who prepares the exhibition, but of a Docent who explains the original patron's needs and the original artists' methods; for it is because of what these patrons and artists were that the works before us are what they are.[5]

Imparting a deeper *raison d'être* of museums, Coomaraswamy elevated the concept to another dimension altogether. Strange it is that in India, a country rich in spiritual and cultural traditions, such an outlook has never developed in our times, nor has there been any deliberations on giving shape to such a vision:

---

[4] *Demands for Grants*, para 50.

[5] Ananda Coomaraswamy, "Why Exhibit Works of Art", in *Christian and Oriental Philosophy of Art*, 1956, p. 8.

> If the exhibition of works of art, like the reading of books, is to have a cultural value, i.e. if it is to nourish and make the best part of us grow, as plants are nourished and grow in suitable soils, it is to the understanding and not to fine feelings that an appeal must be made. In one respect the public is right; it always wants to know what a work of art is "about". . . . Let us tell them the painful truth, that most of these works of art are about God, whom we never mention in polite society. Let us admit that if we are to offer an education in agreement with the innermost nature and eloquence of the exhibits themselves, that this will not be an education in sensibility, but an education in philosophy.[6]

With the aesthetics and philosophy of display missing the artefacts exhibited at the National Museum and in most museums across the country, leave much to be desired. The Parliamentary Committee has highlighted this aspect when it pointed out that out of "206,000 collections with the National Museum only 15,681, constituting 7.61 per cent of the total collections, were on display". It expressed its dissatisfaction with the number and the selection of items put on display and called for efforts to "ensure maximum exposure of our rich and diverse heritage to the people".[7] The percentages of display continue to remain quite dismal – e.g. the Indian Museum (Kolkata) displays only 3.18 per cent of its collection, the National Gallery of Modern Art in Delhi 5.88 per cent and the Victoria Memorial Hall in Kolkata only 5.28 per cent of its total collection. The Art Acquisition Committee of the National Museum has also been lying defunct stalling any serious effort at artefact acquisition and enhancement of the collection.

---

6 Ananda Coomaraswamy, "Why Exhibit Works of Art", in *Christian and Oriental Philosophy of Art*, 1956, p. 20.

7 *One Hundred Seventy Ninth Report on Action Taken by the Government on the Recommendations/Observations of the Committee on the Functioning of the National Museum, 2012*, para 25.

The apathy became further evident when it was disclosed that physical verification of artefacts had "not been done at the National Museum, New Delhi, and National Gallery of Modern Art since 2003 and 2000, respectively". Even if the serious lapse is rectified in future, the damage – perhaps irreparable – may have been done already. The Committee recommended that "for the sake of preserving the invaluable treasures" the government immediately take cognizance of this and initiate immediate steps to address the lapse. A delay in this, the Committee argued, will make the fixing of responsibility for the "missing" and "mishandled" treasures of the nation "a daunting task".[8] In his memoirs, veteran archaeologist, Dilip K. Chakrabarti corroborates much the same point when he says that "museums do not publish the catalogues of the objects they are in charge of. This is plain unadulterated truth".[9] The National Museum, points out Chakrabarti, "has no published catalogue of its sculptures, archaeological materials, etc". It was not so much the lack of manpower that really prevents the drawing up of such a catalogue, he argues, "it is just pure simple laziness to sit at tables and get on with the business".[10]

Another area, where we have allowed neglect to creep in, is epigraphy. Noting a huge vacuum in the field the Parliamentary Committee report has called for an increased capacity building in this field. Such neglect is unthinkable for a country like India, rich in epigraphical sources and material. Even in the mid-1980s the issue had attained criticality but there appears to have been no systematic thinking on it even then. As entire generations of painstaking epigraphists pass away, there is hardly anyone to replace them or take forward

---

[8] *Demands for Grants*, para 55.

[9] Dilip K. Chakrabarti, *Fifty Years of Indian Archaeology*, 2012, p. 311.

[10] Ibid.

their work. In an essay, titled "The Self-Awakening of India: The Context of the Past, the Present and the Future", noted social scientist and historian Dharampal (1922–2006) called for doing "something now" in order to address the neglect of India's vast epigraphical resources. In the light of the present situation it is interesting to read Dharampal's suggestions. An archival scholars *par excellence* of modern India, Dharampal had called for setting up one institution each for various linguistic and cultural regions of India with the requisite expertise:

> These institutions should serve as depositories of all manuscript wealth of the region, or of copies or microfilms of what is not obtainable in the original.[11]

They should also have centres "of inscriptional and epigraphical material, as well as libraries which [should] contain every printed and published item of the particular region, and the more important material in Sanskrit, or any other Indian or foreign language material regarding India's past and civilization". These libraries could house sections that help in understanding other civilizations of the world.[12]

The National Mission for Manuscripts launched in 2003 has salvaged the situation a bit, but much more remains to be done, especially in light of the huge epigraphical material that continues to face neglect and decay. Most Indian archives and libraries, however, continue to face neglect. There is a "glaring dearth of trained archivists and librarians" in such institutions across the country and preservation methods and technologies used in them have "greatly lagged behind what is practised elsewhere in the world". The premier Indian National Archives, for example, is in desperate need of more qualified

---

[11] Dharampal, "The Self-Awakening of India", in *Essays on Tradition, Recovery and Freedom, Collected Writings*, vol. 5, 2000, p. 105.

[12] Ibid.

staff who would assist in preservation and cataloguing. Unless, the Ministry of Culture and the government shake off their apathy and initiate immediate rectifying action, "India is at risk of letting much of its heritage literally crumble into dust".[13] A wide vision, such as elaborated by Dharampal and the determination to implement it at war footing may eventually stem the decay.

Dharampal forcefully argued for the need to extensively review our approach to our culture and heritage. Discussing the role of museums, he argued for paying close attention to "our ancient artefacts, the multiple of tools and design of our civilization".[14] And for this it was necessary to set up artefacts museums in every district of India as centres which would enable people from the area, including students, to get acquainted with their heritage and with how they functioned in the past. The museums, Dharampal observed, could also "have suitable charts to explain matters, and display samples of the productions of these artifacts". Besides this it was necessary to "recognize and strengthen [the] existing regional and national museums" disengaging them from a lot of seventeenth, eighteenth, nineteenth-century "European knick-knacks".[15] The point made may be debatable, but the essential question is whether we have really been able to evolve and design museums which would reflect, illustrate and explain in essence India's cultural and civilizational ethos? Have we really succeeded in weaving in, an education through museums and in applying our mind towards evolving a framework that would instantly strike a chord with young learners and

---

13 Dinyar Patel, "Our Past Is Being Moth-eaten", in *The Hindu*, 19 April 2012.

14 Dharampal, "The Self-Awakening of India", p. 105.

15 Ibid., p. 26.

awaken an yearning in them for a true knowledge of their own culture and civilization?

Parliament, or for that matter other institutions of Indian public life, hardly ever witnesses spirited debates on Indian culture and on the cultural need and direction of the nation. In the absence of such a debate a new direction or a refreshing plan of action in the sphere is therefore unable to emerge.

This was but one, and visible aspect of the apathy that we exude towards our culture. Our thinkers under discussion would have surely been shocked at this neglect of culture by those for whom they spoke. Neglect of culture in other areas in India is a vast subject in itself and it would be difficult to enter into a discussion of its various aspects and dimensions in the present work. However a look at the neglect or apathy towards culture in the vital arena of education gives an idea, an understanding of the magnitude of the neglect and of how we have failed to evolve a coherent teaching framework for culture. Our young minds remain illiterate when it comes to appreciating and absorbing the cultural essence and the myriad cultural expressions of their land.

Culture in Education: The Thirst and The Absence

A 2004 survey on the "Cultural Content at School" commissioned by the National Council of Education Research and Training (NCERT) and undertaken by the Coimbatore-based International Forum for India's Heritage (IFIH) made a startling find: while schools were neglecting cultural education students expressed a deep thirst for it. The survey and the report, now lost among the routine publications of the NCERT, brought out certain fundamental points regarding culture and education in the country. But our apathy has compelled it to remain what it was – a mere report. No known effort has been made to really ascertain whether and how the findings could be translated into an effective educational action.

Its inability to generate a debate is not a reflection on the content or the composition of the report but rather a reflection on our general attitude towards culture. A look at some of the conclusions of the survey supports our position that Indian education woefully lacks a cultural vision and approach. The appeal of the survey is in the fact that it is one of those few which have involved the students themselves.

The massive survey covered "over 11,000 students from all over India and across diverse types of schools and mediums" and provides "first-hand feedback from the students as regards the cultural and value content of the curriculum" of Standards 9th to 12th. Among other things, the students' voice came out clearly in favour of "integrating Indian culture in the curriculum".[16] Learners were asked to give their views on "(1) whether Indian culture is given adequate importance in the curriculum, (2) whether students would like to learn specific aspects of Indian heritage as part of or outside the curriculum", etc.[17]

There was no attempt to enter into a theoretical definition of culture, rather the questionnaire "began with a list of aspects of Indian heritage which any student would relate to on an empirical level". The range of Indian culture offered was wide and included "arts (including music, dance, painting), science (including Indian achievements in mathematics, astronomy, chemistry, medicine), festivals, traditional sports and games, literature (ancient or modern), inspiring historical or mythical characters, yoga and spirituality".[18] The survey's principal

---

16 Michel Danino, "The Voice of Students", in *Journal of Value Education*, vol. 4, nos. 1-2, January-July 2004, p. 124. To be precise the survey covered '11,026 students drawn from 278 schools spread over twenty-one states of India, studying in eight different languages.

17 Ibid., p. 125.

18 Ibid., p. 127.

findings on cultural education continue to retain a capacity to generate debate and also leaves immense scope for cultural innovation and formulation in education in the country:

- ***Learning Indian culture***: Ninety-one per cent of all 11,026 students surveyed felt that they will benefit from learning elements of Indian culture.
- ***In or out of curriculum***: Eighty per cent wished Indian culture to be part of extra-curricular activities, while sixty per cent wanted it taught as part of the curriculum. Forty-five per cent wanted it through both methods.
- ***Aspects of Indian culture***: Among the aspects of Indian culture that students would like to learn, art comes first, followed by *asana*s and *pranayama*, [traditional Indian games like] *kabaddi* came next, followed by meditation.
- ***Indian arts***: Students showed a liking for Bharat-natyam, Carnatic and Hindustani music, despite the fact that art is clearly low on the priorities of today's education: over a third of students had little awareness of Indian art forms, and only 37 per cent reported learning art as part of their regular curriculum.[19]

On festivals, the survey revealed that "hardly a quarter of students were aware of the significance of popular festivals". Eighty-three per cent students found "the practices of *asanas*, *pranayama* and meditation helpful and at least in a positive trend 52 per cent learnt these at school while 28 per cent learnt them outside".[20] Awareness of the traditional Indian texts such as the *Ramayana*, *Mahabharata*, teachings of Buddha

---

[19] Michel Danino, "The Voice of Students", in *Journal of Value Education*, vol. 4, nos. 1-2, January-July 2004, p. 127.

[20] Ibid.

and other saints "came from outside the school".[21] The regional and tribal traditions also seem to have been neglected in general and "only a third of students reported having learned stories or teachings from these".[22] Of languages, a vital cultural parameter, 51 per cent of students surveyed felt that Indian languages (ancient or modern) should be learned, half of them for cultural reasons, the other half for the promotion of national integration.[23]

The other interesting finding of the survey which could deepen the debate, is that Indian language students "value Indian culture (including *yoga* and meditation) markedly more than their English-medium counterparts" and are also more eager to learn it.[24] The movement upward from class 9 to 12, saw a decrease in cultural content and a rise in feeling among students for its need.[25] The school type also provides directions on cultural education, the study found private schools to have "more cultural content than government schools" and it was seen that the demand for "Indian culture to be integrated in the curriculum" was higher among students in government run rural schools.[26] On the whole it was seen that students of rural government schools "showed far more interest in Indian culture, followed by their counterparts from private urban schools". Students of urban government schools "seemed the least" interested in cultural education.[27]

One of the major findings of the survey was that there existed a "substantial degree of interest in Indian culture",

---

21 Michel Danino, "The Voice of Students", pp. 127-28.

22 Ibid., p. 128.

23 Ibid.

24 Ibid.

25 Ibid., p. 129.

26 Ibid.

27 Ibid.

among students revealing an acute thirst for cultural education.[28] Yet the general consensus that "India's school system, a legacy of the colonial era, needs a considerable amount of reform if it is to meet the needs of a modern independent nation with a huge and ever-growing number of students"[29] has remained a consensus without really inspiring any long-term thinking on the issue. The omission of cultural education is just another legacy of India's colonial past. A legacy which has ensured that the fundamentals of Indian culture and civilization remain "non-existent" in the entire educational framework.[30]

The divorce between culture and education remains entrenched. Discussing some aspects of cultural policies in India four decades ago, one of India's leading cultural advocates Kapila Vatsyayan, for example, noted this divorce when she wrote that "in spite of the recommendations of the Education Commission [constituted by the Government of India] for the introduction of an intensive programme which would inculcate social, moral, cultural and spiritual values, much more needs to be done at the school level than has been achieved".[31] Even then fine arts were considered "peripheral to formal education" and were continued to be neglected. Vatsyayan had then complained that this was due to the "lack

---

28 Danino, "The Voice of Students", p. 128.

29 Ibid., p. 124.

30 For a detailed treatment of the subject see e.g. the chapter "Wounded Identity" in Michel Danino's *Indian Culture and India's Future* (2011), especially pp. 185-87. The education system, more importantly a certain perspective of it, made it a habit to reject "the fundamentals of her [India's] civilization and culture", deny "India's cultural continuity and identity" [and] "underemphasize" or ignore "India's civilizational achievements and contributions to world culture" etc. (Ibid., p. 186.)

31 Kapila Vatsyayan, *Some Aspects of Cultural Policies in India*, 1972, p. 27.

of adequate facilities for the training of teachers in music, dance and individual arts" and because of the "difficulty of getting teaching aids easily".[32] The situation may be no different today. Vatsyayan was right in pointing out then and the situation seems to be true today as well that a "large part of cultural training and development continues to be divorced from formal education".[33] What was distressing was the "lack of courses or opportunities for the educational community, both in urban and rural areas, to become initiated into the appreciation of the arts or to participate, in a corporate manner in creative activities such as the crafts".[34] The realization that the cultural content of education or cultural education have to possess a deeper dimension continues to be absent. In Vatsyayan's words:

> The cultural content of education is more than a matter of introduction of courses in the performing, visual and verbal arts and practical crafts: it must permeate the studies of the humanities and result in an expansion of the mental horizons of the narrow specialist; it must also equip the educated to see the interrelationships and interdependence of disciplines, to be rooted in the earth while aspiring for the freedom of the skies.[35]

Pointing at the neglect of "socio-cultural education" in universities in India, Vatsyayan argued that this happened because of the strangle grip of the "outmoded examination system, the narrow one-dimensional teaching of the arts and sciences at the undergraduate level" which made no attempt "to correlate and to ėstablish relationships between the content of various disciplines and the form of various activities" and

---

32 Kapila Vatsyayan, *Some Aspects of Cultural Policies in India*, 1972, p. 27.

33 Ibid., p. 29.

34 Ibid., p. 31.

35 Ibid.

acted as grave impediments to the "cultural growth of the education community".[36] The moot question is whether the situation has changed for the better today. The aim of a cultural education should essentially be to create individuals "who will have the capacity to communicate with the past and to keep pace with the future, to hold the "still centre" of the inner life while continually adapting and renovating outer forms".[37] Has the agenda of cultural education in India tried to fulfil that, or, to put it more plainly, is there an agenda at all?

There is an absence of imaginative initiative in this area of educational planning. In recent years this "cultural desertification" of Indian education seems to have struck a certain section of Indians who have tried to fill this obvious gap by introducing "a course on Indian culture, heritage and ethos". Often this compounds the problem, it "sends a subtle message that Indian culture is a 'separate' topic, unrelated to the others: you learn mathematics, geography, civics *and also* Indian culture". Such an approach only gives credence to the impression that "Indian culture has little to do with mainstream disciplines".[38]

A broad cultural education for the Indian learner could have the following essential aims:

- Integration of values – done through the medium of Indian stories that abound in Indian literature.
- Integration of elements of India's heritage in every discipline – narrating the story of India's civilizational achievements in nearly every modern discipline that the student is introduced to.

---

36 Kapila Vatsyayan, *Some Aspects of Cultural Policies in India*, 1972, p. 31.

37 Ibid., p. 32.

38 Danino, *Integrating India's Heritage in Indian Education*, p. 4.

- Conveying something of the Indian world-view and "show how it is growing more and more relevant in today's world" and inspire the learners to situate themselves in their present world.[39]

The details of such an education need to be urgently worked out and yet there seems to be no concerted initiative to synergize these efforts and develop a comprehensive roadmap. Even if schools and colleges were to introduce elements of cultural education in their curriculum on their own, are there trained teachers to implement it? The present teacher's training packages have hardly any space for such knowledge. So devoid is this training of the cultural aspect that teachers interested in taking the lead in integrating heritage and culture in education have to make a "double effort". They have to make an effort on the one hand, "in familiarizing themselves with India's achievement, of which they are unaware (being themselves 'products of the system')" and such an effort "involves a good deal of training, research and self-education". On the other hand, they have to make an effort in "selecting and putting across some of the material to the students in a way that they feel struck, inspired by, filled with admiration for this ancient and yet living civilization."[40]

Is the present Indian system and framework of teacher's training really geared up to facilitate such innovation, initiative and self-education on the part of the teachers? Does it provide them with the space and the élan to chart out a wide and exciting roadmap for a cultural journey in education?

---

39 Ibid., p. 5. For a more detailed discussion see the paper at: http://www.ifih.org/IntegratingIndiasHeritageinIndianEducation.htm

40 Danino, *Integrating India's Heritage*, p. 15.

Epilogue

Indian Culture : Signposts for the Future

THE observations of the parliamentary panel and the survey on the cultural contents in school provide a disturbing insight into the position of culture in India today. In his essays on the Indian renaissance, written as a spirited defence of Indian culture, Sri Aurobindo described the culture of a people as the "expression of a consciousness of life" which formulated itself in three aspects:

> . . . a side of thought, of ideal, of upward will and the soul's aspiration; . . . a side of creative self-expression and appreciative aesthesis, intelligence and imagination; and . . . a side of practical and outward formulation.[1]

It is high time that we give attention, especially in education, to all these three vital aspects of our cultural expression. The pressing question which remains is how best can one work these out in the national life and how best can one ensure continuity. It is essential to ask these important questions of our direction in culture, if we are not, as Sri Aurobindo once put it, to allow, "our cultural independence to be paralysed".[2]

But the other crucial question is why do we seem to lose the sense of our cultural pervasiveness? Culture once upon a time permeated the life of India, we were not alien to this

---

[1] Sri Aurobindo, "A Defence of Indian Culture", in *CWSA*, vol. 20, p. 106.

[2] Sri Aurobindo, "The Renaissance in India", in *CWSA*, vol. 20, p. 37.

permeation, as a civilization we were used to it, nurtured it and lived it. Compendiums of ancient Indian texts testify the position that in India "socially, culture was not the exclusive right of a small elite revolving around the seat of political power". Often the king and the ruler acted as the "patron-in-chief" and at other times, "highly sophisticated forms were sustained and nurtured through the individual effort of a small group of people subscribing to a particular faith".[3] There was a cultural tradition which was "more pervasive" and which "was shared, promoted and fostered by the will and effort of people of all sections of society, economically privileged and underprivileged".[4] It is essential that we dwell on the dimensions of this pervasiveness, which is still evident but is usually glossed over by a veneer of a so-called modernity. A failure to recognize this, an inability or disinterestedness to dwell on the three essential aspects of culture that Sri Aurobindo so succintly described, a refusal to re-evaluate the cultural positions of some of our early cultural nationalists may perhaps severely challenge our ability to envisage and to eventually work out a cultural continuity. The "Indianness" that our thinkers so animatedly discussed also stands challenged and yet it is in preserving and nurturing this very "Indianness" that culture plays a pivotal and epochal role. India's Indianness is best preserved, as Sri Aurobindo put it, by "being herself and following the law of her own nature". This did not and does not mean:

> As some narrowly and blindly suppose, the rejection of everything new that come to us in the stream of Time or happens to have been first developed or powerfully expressed by the West. Such an attitude would be intellectually absurd, physically impossible, and above all unspiritual; true spirituality rejects no new light, no added

[3] Kapila Vatsyayan, *Some Aspects of Cultural Policies in India*, pp. 11-12.

[4] Ibid., p. 11.

> means or materials of our human self-development. It means simply to keep our centre, our essential way of being, our inborn nature and assimilate to it all we receive, and evolve out of it all we do and create.[5]

But a comprehensive knowledge and feel of this essential way of our being has to come about through an assiduous but not an isolated study of ourselves. As Dharampal pointed out in his essay on India's self-awakening,

> we have to acquire a thorough understanding of our past whether it is reflected through myths or through historically verifiable facts and equally acquire an adequate comprehension, from an Indian perspective, of other civilizations of the world.[6]

In fact, in this age of great and rapid change and bouleversement some of our early cultural nationalists saw the danger, as Sri Aurobindo articulated it in the 1920s, that India's ancient culture, attacked by Western modernism, "overpowered in the material field, [and] betrayed by the indifference of her children" may "perish for ever along with the soul of the nation that holds it in its keeping".[7] It is this attitude of "indifference" that poses the severest challenge to the values and continuity of Indian culture and civilization. The challenge needs to be urgently recognized and evaluated. As Dharampal argued in his discussion of the "Bhāratīya Chitta, Mānas and Kāla," "we need to form a picture of the Indian *Chitta* [inner mind] and *Kāla* [sense of time, epochs], and to place the modern consciousness and modern times within that picture."[8] Sri

---

[5] *The Renaissance in India*, p. 38.

[6] Dharampal, *The Self-Awakening of India*, p. 104.

[7] Sri Aurobindo, "Is India Civilised", in *The Complete Works of Sri Aurobindo* (CWSA), vol. 20, Puducherry: Sri Aurobindo Ashram, 1997, p. 56.

[8] Dharampal, *Bhāratīya Chitta, Mānas and Kāla*, 1993, p. 30.

Aurobindo discussing the renaissance in India talked of the need to adapt to modernity by keeping intact the central civilizational truths. It was such a renaissance that he hoped would work itself out in India. Writing at a time when the cultural nationalist discourse was trying to bring out new forms of expressions, he observed:

> Now that the salvation, the reawakening has come, India will certainly keep her essential spirit, will keep her characteristic soul, but there is likely to be a great change of the body. The shaping for itself of a new body, of new philosophical, artistic, literary, cultural, political, social forms by the same soul rejuvenescent will, I should think, be the type of the Indian renascence–forms not contradictory of the truths of life which the old expressed, but rather expressive of the those truths restated, cured of defect, completed.[9]

But the restating of the old truths through newer expressions remains in danger of being stunted if this indifference towards "India's ancient culture" continues to grow. The newer expressions may then become devoid of the essential civilizational spirit and ethos; they may not reflect this Indianness and only lead to a greater cultural subjection. In his essay "Swaraj in Ideas", Indian philosopher K.C. Bhattacharya had described the dimensions of such a "cultural subjection". Cultural subjection, argued Bhattacharya, is:

> Ordinarily of an unconscious character and it implies slavery from the very start. . . . There is cultural subjection only when one's traditional cast of ideas and sentiments is superseded without comparison or competition by a new cast representing an alien culture which possesses one like a ghost. This subjection is a slavery of the spirit.[10]

9 *The Renaissance in India*, p. 5

10 "Swaraj in Ideas" in *Four Indian Critical Essays*, p. 13.

An abounding manifestation of such a subjection invariably prevents efforts at a renewed exploration and internalization of that Indianness. Are evidences of such subjection not visible around? Are not the new casts of ideas that we, as a civilization, are daily exposed to, being accepted without comparison and competition? Bhattacharya had lamented that the Indian mind had ceased to, or "dares not exert itself in the cultural sphere" and deprecated the fact that there was no "vigorous output of Indian contribution in a distinctive Indian style to the culture and thought of the modern world".[11] The problem, he noted, was with "our education", it had "not so far helped us to understand ourselves, to understand the significance of our past, the realities of our present and our mission of the future. It has tended to drive our real mind into the unconscious and to replace it by a shadow mind that has no roots in our past and in our real present".[12] Such a confusion had only served to bring about the "hybridization" of our ideas, and this, contended Bhattacharya, "is one of the most distressing features of our present situation".[13] The inability to express ourselves on our terms inspired by the essentials of our culture, our tradition, our *parampara,* remains a task unaddressed. One asks if such a situation has altered for the better today, or whether it has altered at all? The crisis, Bhattacharya argued, was that, while we were well acquainted with the principles and details of Western life and thought, we had not, or were yet to

> sufficiently realize where we actually stand today and how to apply our bookish principles to our situation in life. We either accept or repeat the judgements passed on us by Western culture, or we impotently resent them but have

[11] "Swaraj in Ideas" in *Four Indian Critical Essays*, p. 14.

[12] Ibid., p. 16.

[13] Ibid., p. 17.

> hardly any estimates of our own, wrung from an inward perception of the realities of our position.[14]

Such a position may be dismissed as relevant only to situations in a colonial India, but one cannot completely shake off the residual feeling that it does continue to reflect present situations as well. Is there a comprehensive effort at an authentic reappropriation of our cultural space?[15] In fact, as I have argued, our nationalist thinkers were quite confirmed in their view that there was indeed "no contradiction between being culturally rooted and being a global citizen". Such a conviction drove them to advocate the need for us to be first rooted within our cultural essentials; they foresaw, unlike a majority of their compatriots then, that, "photocopies are not respected"[16] and had realized that:

> in a world of cultural asymmetry and one where the pressures of co-option are immense, individual cultures have to make extra efforts to preserve *and* project their distinct heritage and way of life.[17]

For the once colonized, who had to face a concerted and continuous onslaught on their essential way of being and expression, so that a deliberate "decline of . . . confidence and intellect"[18] could be engineered, and who were in a sense "robbed . . . of the pride and security that come from being rooted",[19] this "extra-effort" is what is needed today to restate that Indianness and to arrest the decline in cultural values and the faith in its essentials. As Dharampal had movingly stated:

---

14 "Swaraj in Ideas" in *Four Indian Critical Essays*, p. 15.

15 Pavan K. Varma, *Becoming Indian*, 2010, p. 255.

16 Ibid., p. 258.

17 Ibid.

18 Dharampal, op. cit., p. 73.

19 *Becoming Indians*, op. cit., p. 258.

> The self-awakening of India is bound to remain similarly elusive and transient till we find a secure basis for a confident expression of Indian civilization within the modern world and the modern epoch. We must establish a conceptual framework that makes Indian ways and aspirations seem viable in the present, so that we do not feel compelled or tempted to indulge in demeaning imitations of the modern world, and the people of India do not have to suffer humiliation of seeing their ways and their seekings being despised in their own country. . . .[20]

As he had cautioned in the 1920s,[21] Sri Aurobindo's concern with the "Indianness" of India continued right till the end, in fact by December 1950, when he passed away, Sri Aurobindo had outlived most of the early thinkers in our discussion. But he was speaking for all of them when he expressed that concern in one of his last public addresses in December 1948. He pointed at the spiritual-cultural moorings of Indian civilization and the challenge ahead:

> There are deeper issues for India herself, since by following certain tempting directions she may conceivably become a nation like many others evolving an opulent industry and commerce, a powerful organization of social and political life, an immense military strength, practising power-politics with a high degree of success, guarding and extending zealously her gains and her interests, dominating even a large part of the world, but in this apparently magnificent progression forfeiting its *Svadharma*, losing its soul. Then ancient India and her spirit might disappear altogether and we would have only

20 Dharampal, op. cit., p. 30.

21 He had expressed his apprehensions of a "Westernised" India turning into a "brown ape of Europe" and passing "into the mould of occidental modernism." Such a turn of events, he cautioned, would lead to the perishing of "ancient India" altogether. ("Is India Civilized", p. 73.)

> one more nation like the others and that would be a real gain neither to the world nor to us.[22]

Unless, "undeterred by the cavillings of an alien mind", the "sense of grandeur and beauty" and "inner significance"[23] of the achievements of Indian culture and civilization are recovered, the best hopes for the future shall remain unrealized. Our cultural dimensions and expressions are sure indicators of an essential civilizational repositioning. And the revisiting of the debate on Indian culture is therefore necessary to form that picture of the Indian essence, the essential way of being, of the Indianness and to situate ourselves culturally and civilizationally today in the wider world. The cultural sub-text of the whole of Indian civilization needs candid reflection and the ideational dimensions of the cultural debate in India can provide us with a sense and a direction towards forming the essential texture of Indianness.

Generating and sustaining the debate on culture in India and unraveling anew its dimensions remain one of the best paths towards recovering that deeper significance and the exploration of past dimensions of that debate is but a step towards that unraveling. If in the years to come India aspires to play a considerable global role along with the rise of other non-Western cultures, it has then been rightly argued that the "need to explicate what it means to be an Indian (and what the 'Indianness' of Indian culture consists of) will soon [have to] become the task of the entire intelligentsia in India."[24] A

---

22 Sri Aurobindo, "Message to Andhra University", in *Autobiographical Notes and Other Writings of Historical Interest*, 2006, pp. 503-04.

23 Sri Aurobindo, "Defence of Indian Culture", in *The Complete Works of Sri Aurobindo* (CWSA), vol. 20, Puducherry: Sri Aurobindo Ashram, 1997, p. 297.

24 S.N. Balagangadhara, "Foreword" to *Invading the Sacred: An Analysis of Hinduism Studies in America*, 2007, p. vii.

response to the understanding of India will have to be generated. Such a response will be required "because the theoretical and textual study of the Indian culture has been undertaken mostly by the West in the last three hundred years"[25] within a cultural framework that was generated from another clime and another perception. Most of our cultural nationalists were the early pioneers of the effort at evolving such a response. They began formulating an explication through seeking to rejuvenate the Indian mind and life by "irrigating it with the waters of [her] tradition"[26] and of her culture. That attempt must now gather greater momentum and continue unabated.

---

[25] S.N. Balagangadhara, "Foreword" to *Invading the Sacred: An Analysis of Hinduism Studies in America*, 2007, p. vii.

[26] Arvind Sharma, "Foreword" to *The Essential Ananda K. Coomaraswamy*, 2004, p. xi.

Bibliography

Aurobindo, Sri, *Autobiographical Notes and Other Writings of Historical Interest*, Puducherry: Sri Aurobindo Ashram, rpt., 2006.

——— *The Renaissance in India and Other Essays on Indian Culture*, Puducherry: Sri Aurobindo Ashram, 1997.

Baedeker, Karl, *Greece: Handbook for Travellers*, Leipsic: Karl Baedeker, Publisher, 2nd rev. edn., 1894.

Basu, Sankari Prasad, *Nivedita Lokmata*, vol. 4, Kolkata: Ananda Publishers, 1401 [Beng].

——— , *Vivekananda O Samakalin Bharatbarsha* [Vivekananda and Contemporary India], vols. 1-7, Kolkata: Mondal Book House, 6th imp., 2009.

Bhattacharya, K.C., "Swaraj in Ideas", in S.K.Ghosh (ed.) *Four Indian Critical Essays*, Kolkata: Jijnasa, 1977.

Burke, Marie Louis, *Swami Vivekananda in the West: New Discoveries*, vols. 1-6, Kolkata: Advaita Ashrama, 4th edn., 1998.

Calvé Emma, My Life (trans. Rosamond Gilder), New York: D. Appleton and Co., 1922.

Chakrabarti, Dilip K., *Colonial Indology: Sociopolitics of the Ancient Indian Past*, New Delhi: Munshiram Manoharlal, 1997.

——— , *Fifty Years of Indian Archaeology: Journey of a Foot Soldier*, New Delhi: Aryan Books International, 2012.

Complete Works of Sister Nivedita (CWSN), vols. 3, 4 and 5, Kolkata: Advaita Ashrama.

Complete Works of Swami Vivekananda (CWSV), vols. 3, 5 and 8, Kolkata: Advaita Ashrama, Mayavati Memorial Edition.

Complete Works of Sri Aurobindo (CWSA), vols. 1 and 20, Puducherry: Sri Aurobindo Ashram Publication Department.

Coomaraswamy, Ananda, *Art and Swadeshi*, Madras: Ganesh & Co. , 1911.

——— , *Christian and Oriental Philosophy of Art*, New York: Dover Publication, 1956.

———, *Essays in National Idealism*, Madras: G.A. Natesan & Co., 1909.

———, *The Bugbear of Literacy*, London: Dennis Dobson, 1946.

———, *The Dance of Shiva*, New York: The Sunwise Turn, 1918.

Coomaraswamy, Rama P. (ed.), *The Essential Ananda K. Coomaraswamy*, Indiana: World Wisdom, 2004.

Cousens Henry, "Somanatha and other Mediaeval Temples in Kathiawad", in *Archaeological Survey of India*, vol. XLV, Imperial Series, Calcutta: Government of India Central Publication Branch, 1931.

Danimo, Mitchel, *Indian Culture and India's Future*, New Delhi: D.K. Printworld, 2011.

———, "Integrating India's Heritage with Indian Education", paper presented at the National Symposium on Cultural Education in 21st Century India, Amrita Vishwa Vidyapeetham, Ettimadai, May 2004.

Das Sisir Kumar (ed.), *The English Writings of Rabindranath Tagore*, vols. 1-2, New Delhi: Sahitya Akademi, repr., 2008.

Datta, Bhupendranath, *Swami Vivekananda Patriot-Prophet*, Kolkata: Nababharat Publishers, 1954.

Dharampal, *Collected Writings*, vols. 1-5, Goa: Other India Press, 2000.

Dharampal, *Bhāratīya Chitta, Mānas and Kāla* (trans. Jitendra Bajaj). Chennai: Centre for Policy Studies, 1993.

Dutt, R.C., *A History of Civilisation in Ancient India*, vols. 1-2, London: Kegan Paul, Trench Trubner & Co., 1893.

Fergusson, James, *History of Indian and Eastern Architecture*, vols. 1-2, London: John Murray, rev. edn., 1910.

Gopal, S. (ed.), *Selected Works of Jawaharlal Nehru (SWJN)*, 2nd Series, vol. 10, 1990; vol. 14, pt. II, New Delhi: Jawaharlal Nehru Memorial Fund, 1995.

Goswami, Kunja Gobinda, *Excavations at Bangarh* (1938-41), Calcutta: University of Calcutta, 1948.

Jawaharlal Nehru Speeches, vol. 2, 1949-53, New Delhi: The Publication Division, Ministry of Information and Broadcasting, Government of India, 1954.

Kumar, Ravindra, H.Y. Sharada Prasad (ed.), *SWJN*, 2nd Series, vol. 25, New Delhi: Jawaharlal Nehru Memorial Fund, 1999.

———, H.Y. Sharada Prasad (ed.), *SWJN*, 2nd Series, vol. 28, New Delhi: Jawaharlal Nehru Memorial Fund, 2001.

Letters of Swami Vivekananda, Kolkata: Advaita Ashrama, 16th imp., 2007.

Madhok, Balraj, *Dr. Syamaprasad Mookerjee: A Biography*, New Delhi: Deepak Prakashan, 1954.

Mahaffy, J.P., *Rambles and Studies in Greece*, Philadelphia: The John C. Winston Co., 1892.

Mitra, Rajendralal, *Indo-Aryans: Contributions Towards the Elucidation of the Ancient and Mediaeval History*, vols. 1-2, London: Edward Stanford, 1881.

Mookerjee, Radhakumud, *Nationalism in Hindu Culture*, London: Theosophical Publishing House, 1921.

Mukherjee, Haridas and Uma, *The Origins of the National Education Movement*, Kolkata: National Council of Education, repr., 2000.

Munshi, K.M., *Foundations of Indian Culture*, Bombay: Bharatiya Vidya Bhavan, 1974.

———, *Pilgrimage to Freedom*, Bombay: Bharatiya Vidya Bhavan, 1967.

———, *Somanatha the Shrine Eternal*, Bombay: Bharatiya Vidya Bhavan, 1965.

Nehru, Jawaharlal, *The Discovery of India*, New Delhi: Oxford University Press, 1985.

———, *Toward Freedom*, New York: John Day & Co., 1941.

Nivedita, Sister and Ananda Coomaraswamy, *Myths of the Hindus and Buddhists*, London: George G. Harrap & Co., repr., 1920.

Nivedita, Sister, *Footfalls of Indian History*, London: Longmans, Green and Co., 1915.

———, *Notes on Some Wandering with the Swami Vivekananda* (edited by Swami Saradananda), Kolkata: Udbodhan Office, 1913.

———, *Selected Essays*, Madras: Ganesh & Co., 1911.

———, *The Master as I Saw Him*, London: Longmans, Green & Co., 1910.

Patel, Manibehn Vallabhbhai and G.M. Nandurkar (eds.), *Sardar Patel's Letters: Mostly Unknown* (1950), vol. 3, Ahmedabad: Sardar Vallabhbhai Patel Smarak Bhavan, 1983.

Ramaswamy, Krishnan, Antonio de Nicolas and Aditi Banerjee (eds.), *Invading the Sacred: An Analysis of Hinduism Studies in America*, New Delhi: Rupa & Co., 2007.

Rao, Amiya and B.G., *Six Thousand Days: Jawaharlal Nehru Prime Minister*, New Delhi: Sterling Publishers, 1974.

Singhal, D.P., *Nationalism in India and Other Historical Essays*, Delhi: Munshiram Manoharlal, 1967.

———, *India and World Civilization*, vols. 1-2, Michigan: Michigan State University Press, 1969.

The Life of Swami Vivekananda by His Eastern and Western Disciples, vols. 1 & 2, Kolkata: Advaita Ashrama, 6th edn., 1989.

Varma, Pavan K., *Becoming India: The Unfinished Revolution of Culture and Identity*, New Delhi: Allen Lane, Penguin, 2010.

Vatsyayan, Kapila, *Some Aspects of Cultural Policies in India*, Paris: Unesco, 1972.

Vidyatmananda, Swami, *Vivekananda in Europe*, Kolkata: Advaita Ashrama, 2012.

Woodroffe, John, *Bharata Shakti*, Madras: Ganesh & Co., 3rd edn., 1921.

———, *Is India Civilised?*, Madras: Ganesh & Co., 1922.

———, *Seed of Race: An Essay on Indian Education*, Madras: Ganesh & Co., 1919.

Report/Journals

Current Science, vol. 94 no. 3, 10 February 2008, Bangalore: Current Science Association, pp. 394-401.

Department Related Parliamentary Standing Committee – One Hundred Seventy Ninth Report on Action Taken by the Government on the Recommendations/ Observations of the Committee Contained in Its One Hundred Sixty Seventh Report on "Functioning of National Museum", New Delhi: Rajya Sabha Secretariat, May 2012.

Department Related Parliamentary Standing Committee on Transport, Tourism and Culture – 175th Report on Demands for Grants (2012-13) of Ministry of Culture, New Delhi: Rajya Sabha Secretariat, May 2012.

Journal of Value Education, vol. 4 nos. 1-2, New Delhi: National Council of Educational Research and Training, 2004.

Shigemi, Inaga, "Sister Nivedita and Her Kali, The Mother: The Web of Indian Life, and Art Criticism: New Insights into Okakura Kakuzo's Indian Writings and the Function of Art in the Shaping of Indian Nationality", in *Japan Review*, 2004, 16: 129-59, Kyoto: International Research Centre for Japanese Studies.

Standing Committee on External Affairs Demands for Grants (2012-13) – 14th Report, New Delhi: Lok Sabha Secretariat, May 2012.

The Vedanta Kesari, Annual Number, vol. 88, December 2001, Chennai: Sri Ramakrishna Math.

The Vedanta Kesari, vol. 37 no. 6, Oct 1950, Madras: Sri Ramakrishna Math.

Private Papers

Syamaprasad Mookerjee Private Papers (SPMPP), Subject File: 21 & 60, Nehru Memorial Museum & Library (NMML), New Delhi.

Index